WILL YOUR DOG
REINCARNATE?

GAIL GRAHAM PHD

ISBN : 1497532876
ISBN 13: 9781497532878

To Jeannie, who was always there for me

INTRODUCTION

Have you lost a beloved pet? Wouldn't it be wonderful if your dog – or cat, or other companion animal – could somehow come back to you? Wouldn't you give just about anything to hold him (or her) in your arms again?

It can happen. It **is** happening. Every day, people like you are being reunited with a cherished dog or cat.

I know, because I'm one of them. My beloved Bao came back to me. He's sitting at my feet as I write this. You don't have to be a mystic or a psychic for this to happen to you. (I'm a retired Professor of Management) You don't even have to believe in reincarnation. But you do need an open mind.

When human beings reincarnate, they are reborn as infants and therefore cannot resume the relationships they enjoyed in previous lives. But dogs are different. Because their life span is so much shorter than ours, our dogs can and do return to us.

Of course, not all dogs return to their owners. When they do, it is because a special bond exists between that dog and that person, a karmic bond that transcends death. Do you and your dog share this kind of special bond? Probably you do. You are reading this book because you are meant to read it.

Some dogs find their way back on their own. But usually, it's a joint effort. The first – and perhaps most challenging step – is realizing that you are a vital part of the equation. You are more powerful than you think. Everything you think and do and say makes a difference.

So what should you be thinking and doing and saying if you want your dog to reincarnate? Basically, all you need to do is reach out to him and let him know that you love him, miss him and want him to come home. Love isn't complicated and neither is reincarnation.

There are many things you can do to help your dog find his way back to you. None of these things are difficult. On the other hand, it isn't merely a question of following a map, or a set of instructions. Every dog is different. Every owner is different. Every relationship is different.

You must trust yourself, especially your instincts. We live in a world of facts and data, and we expect things to make sense. But sometimes, they don't. Knowing and believing are two very different things. You're accustomed to trusting what you know. Now you must learn to trust what you believe. Accepting what you don't understand creates a universe of limitless potential, where anything can happen.

Does it all sound a little bit crazy? In a sense, it is. It involves losing your mind – your rational, critical, reasoning, analytical left brain. It involves believing, rather than knowing. Your mind is important, but you are not your mind. You are something else, something bigger.

Albert Einstein said: There are two ways to live your life – as if nothing is a miracle, and as if everything is a miracle.

Let's make a miracle.

CHAPTER 1

My family was gone and Bao was all I had left. We were inseparable, and we'd been through so much together. Friends worried. If anything happened to Bao, how would I handle it? Bao was my whole life.

He was eleven when he got sick. He wouldn't eat, and over several weeks, he lost nearly a quarter of his body weight. He became so weak he could hardly stand up long enough to pee. His tests results were inconclusive and nobody could figure out what was wrong, but our wonderful veterinarian Dr. Mike Soltero somehow pulled him through.

Just when we thought he was out of the woods, he experienced a pericardial effusion, a buildup of fluid in the sac that holds the heart. The fluid was drained, and sent away for testing. The results were negative for cancer. It can happen once and never happen again, Dr. Mike told me. But six weeks later, it did happen again. And again, four weeks after that. Something was very wrong. More tests were ordered and this time, the fluids tested 90% positive for a rare and very aggressive type of cancer that didn't show up on scans or ultrasounds.

Meanwhile, the pericardial effusions had become weekly occurrences. Something had to be done. The most common treatment – and the most effective, when the underlying cause isn't cancer – is a surgical procedure to cut a "window" in the pericardium which allows the accumulated fluids to drain into the pleural cavity, where they are more easily reabsorbed.

Mercifully, Bao wasn't in any pain. Except for the fact that he tired quickly, you wouldn't know anything was wrong with him. He was his usual, happy little self, living his happy little life. I put off the surgery for a few weeks, hoping the pericardial effusions might go away as quickly as they'd appeared. But they didn't.

On the advice of both Dr. Mike and Bao's cardiologist Dr. Chris Paige we drove to the Colorado State University Veterinary Hospital in Fort Collins for the procedure. Bao was delighted. He loved car trips. He loved motels. He loved traveling. The night before his surgery, I gave him a special dinner, with bones. Right up to the moment they sedated him, he was enjoying his life.

The surgery went on for hours. It was much worse than anyone had thought. Lesions on Bao's pericardium had caused it to adhere to his heart. And there were nodules everywhere, even on his diaphragm. I could tell they didn't think he'd make it through the surgery, but he did. I stayed until he'd awakened from the anesthesia and was wobbling around his little cage. I'd brought one of his soft toys along, and he curled up on top of it and drowsed off. The next 24 hours were critical, I was told. Go back to your motel and get some rest. We'll call you if anything goes wrong.

The telephone rang at midnight. It was Dr. Lana, who was overseeing Bao's care. Bao was in cardiac arrest. They were working on him, trying to bring him back. It isn't good, said Dr. Lana. You'd better come. I drove frantically through the dark, unfamiliar streets. I even ran a red light – the first time in my life I've ever done that. I was in the hospital parking lot when my cell phone rang. It was Dr. Lana. I'm sorry, she said. He's gone.

I was too late. I couldn't even say goodbye. Dr. Lana led me through darkened rooms and silently swinging doors to the hospital section. It had all happened so quickly. I was stunned, numb with shock.

"Is there anyone you can call?" Dr. Lana asked.

It was just past midnight. I called my friend Jeannie, in Scottsdale. I knew she'd be there for me, despite it being the middle of the night. And she was. She picked up before the second ring. It was almost as if she knew.

"He's gone."

"No," says Jeannie. "No, no, no. He can't be dead. He wasn't meant to die. This isn't what was supposed to happen."

They let me hold Bao for nearly an hour. He was still warm. He might have been asleep. The doctors were crying, and I was crying, too. Dr. Lana kept saying, This is the last thing that anyone expected. They let me cut off a lock of his hair, and we made a plaster impression of his dear little paw. And then I went back to the motel, without him.

I wrote in my journal:

> *Bao is gone. The doctors said this was the last thing anybody had expected – that's why they didn't have me come in earlier. He was coping and then suddenly his heart stopped, without warning – he was hooked up to monitors, there was no arrhythmia, his heart just stopped. And they couldn't bring him back, no matter how hard they tried. Oh, Bao – I love you so much, we shared so much, we had so many good times If I'd got there in time, could I have called you back?*

I undress and creep back into bed. After I turn out the light I just lie there, staring into the darkness, still dazed. That's when it happens. That's when I know Bao is coming back to me. He is dead, yes. But he will be reborn, his loving soul in a new, healthy body. He is coming back to me. He is already on his way.

I don't hear a voice. I don't see an image. There is no clap of thunder, no burning bush. It's like a whiff of incense or a shooting star that you can only see out of the corner of your eye, something you might easily miss if you weren't paying attention. I feel it viscerally, although it only lasts for an instant. Then it's gone. But whatever it was, I know it was real. There is no doubt in my mind about that. Bao is coming back to me.

Now I feel as if I'm in the eye of a storm, where the sky is blue and the sun is shining and the storm itself seems impossible. Bao's death is impossible. It's a bad dream. It didn't happen. When I wake up, he'll be here beside me, just as he always is. I close my eyes.

And he **is** beside me when I wake up. Not physically, of course. Bao is gone, I know that. My eyes are red and swollen. I must have been crying all night, even in my sleep. I feel terrible, terrible pain, unbearable loss. Yet I also feel Bao's spirit trying to comfort me, I feel his psychic presence. He is dead, yes. But somehow, he is also here in bed with me.

I was twelve in 1953, when Morey Bernstein hypnotized Virginia Tighe at a cocktail party. It was supposed to be a joke. But under hypnosis Tighe – to everyone's amazement – described her former life in Ireland as Bridey Murphy, a woman who'd lived 200 years earlier. Bernstein wrote a book about it, the book became a best seller and *Life* magazine called the subsequent craze for 'parlor hypnosis" that swept the United States a "hypnotizzy". People threw "come as you were parties" and my mother was convinced that in her former life, she'd been Princess Anastasia.

To me and my friends, reincarnation made as much sense as anything else. It was certainly no more incredible than atomic bombs, television and flying saucers. Although I eventually ceased to believe in the monotheistic deity to whom I said my nightly, childhood prayers, I've never seen anything intrinsically unreasonable in the concept of reincarnation. Everything in the universe follows a cycle of birth, death and rebirth. Why should we be an exception?

I don't remember any of my previous lives. But most people don't, and I've always been unremarkable, parapsychologically speaking. Angels don't talk to me. I see no visions. I hear no voices. In shamanic drumming circles, I'm the one whose animal guide doesn't appear. Yet I remain a Mulder, rather than a Scully. I want to believe.

And I do believe I've lived other lives, even if I don't remember them. I believe we are all part of a gigantic, timeless, cosmic dance in which everything in the universe is connected to everything else and everything we do – or fail to do – in each of our many lives makes a difference. Feelings become thoughts, thoughts become actions and actions become destiny. I believe that at every moment, each of us is changing everything for ourselves and everyone else.

Believing is one thing, but living one's day to day life is something else. Certainly, my belief in reincarnation was of no comfort to me when my husband Rollyn died. I knew that in this lifetime Rollyn and I would never again be together as husband and wife, and reincarnation couldn't change that. Yes, we'd probably meet again in some future life, but what good was that?

This was different. Bao was coming back to me, in this life. I knew it as surely as I knew it was Friday morning and that I was sitting on a bed in a motel room in Fort Collins, Colorado.

Was I simply using a psychological defense mechanism to protect myself from unbearable grief? That's what some people might say. But I disagree. Psychological defense mechanisms are supposed to protect you from pain, and I was in terrible pain. I was heartbroken, overwhelmed by grief, despair, and loss. Knowing that Bao was coming back to me did nothing to ease the heartbreak of having lost him. That might not make sense, but that's how it was.

I had to return to the hospital before I went home. I needed to pay the bill, and I also had an appointment with Veterinary Hospital Clinical Coordinator Gail Bishop, who'd offered me so much encouragement and support yesterday. Was it only yesterday?

A part of my mind still will not accept what has happened, or that Bao is gone. And in a sense, he isn't gone. When I open the car door, I feel him jump in – just as he always does – and curl up on the passenger seat.

"He's still here," I tell Gail. "His spirit is still here. I can feel him. This morning, he was right there in the room with me. And in the car, just now. I can't see him, but I can feel him."

"Is he here in the room with us?"

I shake my head. "But he's waiting for me in the car."

7

Yesterday, I'd told Gail I couldn't imagine a life without Bao. Not surprisingly, she is now concerned about me. She is even more concerned when I tell her I've decided to start back to Scottsdale immediately.

Dr. Lana joins us, and we talk about what happened. "Nobody expected this," Dr. Lana says again. "It's the very last thing we expected. The first 24 hours after surgery are always critical, but he seemed to be doing well. We thought he was going to make it. We are just all so very, very sorry."

There is a moment of silence. Everyone looks so sad. "He's coming back to me. He'll reincarnate," They stare at me. "And he'll be a Shih Tzu again. I don't know if he'll be a boy or a girl. I don't know what he'll look like, either. But I know he's coming back to me."

I'm as astonished as they are. I can't believe I've said such a thing out loud. Their expressions don't change. They don't disagree, or even argue. Of course, I think, they're professionals. This is a veterinary hospital. They're having to deal with this all the time. Animals come here because they're hurt or sick, and some of them don't make it. Most likely, they think I'm in denial. That's the first stage of the grief process – denial.

But I know Bao is gone. I know he is dead. I know I will never feel his warm little body snuggled against me again, never feel the warm rasp touch of his tongue on my face, never watch him joyously work a bone. Just hours ago, I held his motionless little body in my arms, and felt the warmth slowly leave it. No, I am not in denial.

I'm not angry, either. (Anger is the second stage of the grief process) Everything that could be done was done. Thankfully, money had not been an issue. He'd had the best. I have nothing to reproach myself for. There is nothing more I could have done. There is nothing more any of the many doctors could have done, either. If anything, I feel gratitude towards all the kind and dedicated people – in Scottsdale and here in Colorado – who worked so hard and cared so much.

Bargaining is the third stage of the grief process. So am I bargaining? Am I telling myself that it's okay for Bao to be dead so long as it's only temporary? I think about this, walking across the hospital parking lot to my car. But it doesn't feel right. I'm not bargaining. Besides, knowing that Bao is coming back does not mitigate the unbearable pain of having lost him.

It's nearly noon before I begin the long drive back to Scottsdale. Bao's leash and harness are on the passenger's seat next to me, where Bao should have been. But Bao is gone. And yet, he isn't. He is here with me, in the car. Not physically, of course. But his soul, his spiritual essence, is still very close and very real to me. I know he is physically dead, but I also know he was with me in the motel room just now, watching as I packed our things, accompanying me to the car, and then hopping in beside me.

He isn't a ghost, although I know people sometimes believe they've seen their dog's ghost, especially in the first days after death. Every morning until the day he died, artist Murray Urquhart's dog Judy jumped onto his bed and barked – even though Judy herself had passed away 35 years earlier. These things happen. But I can't see Bao, not the way Murray Urquhart saw Judy. I can't hear him, either. His presence is just that – a presence.

Years ago my husband and I spent four weeks in Europe, having left our beloved Dalmatian puppy Rosie at a boarding kennel. One morning in Paris, she was suddenly there in the bed with us. Not as a ghost, but as a palpable – although invisible – presence. We were puzzled. But this was before the days of internet, and it was only when we returned home that we learned she'd died suddenly and quite unexpectedly of massive kidney failure caused by a previously undetected congenital defect. The time of her death corresponded exactly with when we'd felt her there in bed beside us.

Bao's psychic presence resembles Rosie's, but it's much stronger. I can feel him here on the seat next to me, as real to me as my own body and being. He is already on his way back to me. I know it. I can feel it. Yet I'm not comforted by this knowledge, not at all. I can't imagine how I am going to manage without Bao. I don't want to manage without him. I don't want to live without him.

It takes 15 hours to drive from Fort Collins to Scottsdale. South of Denver I drive more or less mindlessly. The road is long and straight and there isn't much traffic. Moving in air-conditioned solitude and silence through mile after mile of empty Colorado high country, I slip into an almost dreamlike state of leaden unhappiness.

I always thought we'd die together. My friends hated it when I said that. But they had husbands and children and grandchildren, and all I had was Bao. And now he is gone. I can't imagine a life without him. I don't want to imagine it.

I think about how easy it would be to put an end to it, here on this deserted, winding mountain road. A sudden twist of the steering wheel, that's all it needs. I have no unfinished business. My affairs are in order. Nobody will miss me. There's nobody left to miss me.

Yet here's Bao, curled up in his usual place on the passenger seat. It doesn't make sense, that he can be dead and also be here. I want to die, I want this awful pain to stop. But I can't, not with Bao sitting here beside me.

As the hours pass, I continue to be aware of his psychic presence. Looking back, I suspect that if someone else had been in the car with me, I might not have felt this presence so strongly. I might have tried to ignore it, or even allowed myself to be talked out of it. But I am alone, and I don't want Bao to leave me.

Now and then, I reach across to stroke his sleeping head, as I often do when we're on the road like this. He is here, but he isn't. I can accept this without understanding it. I'm glad I can accept it. But I'm also glad I don't have to try to explain it to anyone else.

Later, I learn that many people have similar experiences. Sometimes, the sensation that their dog is somehow "there" lasts for days. "But you know it's impossible," one of them told me. "You know your dog is dead. You know that whatever you think you're seeing or sensing can't be real. So you keep busy. You try to ignore it. And after a while, it stops."

Bao stays with me, and I am too exhausted to care if it is impossible or not. The sun moves across the cloudless sky, from east to west, and I drift. I feel as if I'm floating in space, suspended in time with invisible forces and impulses and energies humming all around me. There is no past and no future, only this present moment, this car moving along this road.

Late that afternoon, I become aware that Bao is already a microscopic bundle of dividing cells in a womb. I can't call it a vision, because it isn't a vision. Nor is it a thought. It is more like a realization, something I hadn't known a moment ago but know now. How is this possible? How is any of it possible?

I find myself remembering the time my father brought home a crystal radio set. He let me watch while he set it up and then he showed me how to search for radio frequencies. I turned the dial as slowly and carefully as I could, but nothing happened. Then suddenly, I "got" something. I thought it was magic, until my father explained how crystal radios worked.

That's what I need now, I think. An explanation. I need someone to tell me how this works. Wittgenstein once said, All I know is what I have words for.

Where, I wonder, are the words for this?

Psychologist William James described mystical experiences as being ineffable, noetic, and transient. Is that what this is? Am I finally having an honest-to-goodness mystical experience? According to a National Opinion Research Center survey (Chicago, 1987) 43 percent of all Americans say they've had one. So why shouldn't I?

Many of these people actively seek such experiences, employing techniques like hypnosis, sleep deprivation, chanting and meditation. Others take hallucinogenic drugs. A few – Zen Renzai novices, for example – use extreme pain to shock themselves into insight. But a certain percentage of mystical experiences occur spontaneously, triggered by pain or extreme danger. "Some people awaken spiritually without ever coming into contact with any meditation technique or any spiritual teaching," says Eckhart Tolle. "They may awaken because they can't stand the suffering anymore."

Yet I'm no mystic. I'm not even particularly spiritual. I've never thought of myself in those terms, and I still don't. I'm more comfortable with the crystal radio analogy. Somehow, I've tuned in. The channels are open and the message is coming through. My terrible grief plus the solitude imposed by this long, monotonous journey have combined to create ... what?

A mystical experience? Or a psychotic break?

Again, I reach out to touch Bao and for a moment, I can literally feel his little head. But only for a moment.

I drive on. The sun sinks lower in the sky. The silent knowledge that Bao is on his way back to me does not ease the pain, but it's there, and it is strong as ever. I shake my head. None of it makes sense. And it hurts so much.

HOW TO HELP YOUR DOG REINCARNATE: WEEK ONE

Begin by setting an intention. You want (your dog's name) to come back to you. That's what you want, and that is what is going to happen. Now say it out loud. Say, I want (your dog's name) to come back to me, and he will.

You only need to say it once. Intention is like a spotlight, directing and focussing attention. Where attention goes, energy flows. And when energy flows, things start to happen.

Setting an intention is not like praying. You are not asking for anything. You are making a positive statement about what you want and intend. You want (your dog's name) to come back to you.

But suppose you've never had that strong conviction – as I did – that your dog is going to reincarnate? Does that mean he won't? Not necessarily. Remember, my first perceptions were fleeting and ephemeral. And when I experienced them, I was alone. Had I been distracted by people comforting me or tasks that had to be completed or children who needed to be taken to soccer practice, I'd have probably dismissed the whole thing as imagination, or wishful thinking.

Look at it this way. Something made you pick up this book. Something made you read this far. Messages come in many forms, and there are no coincidences.

It doesn't matter if your dog died yesterday, or last month, or even ten years ago. His spiritual essence still exists, in one or another dimension of the universe. He may be waiting for you to tell him you want him to come back. Or he may have already reincarnated, and is trying to find his way back into your life. If you're thinking about him and wishing he would come back to you, he probably will. Many heartbroken pet parents unconsciously bring their dogs (or cats) back to them in just this way, by continually thinking about them, and remembering them.

But isn't it unhealthy to dwell on things like this? Wouldn't it be better to simply "accept your loss" and move on? In some cases, yes. The exigencies of human biology – for example – make it impossible for us to reunite with a deceased parent or partner in this lifetime. But dogs are different. Their lifespan is much shorter than ours. Dogs and other companion animals can – and do – come back to us. Sometimes the karma is so powerful they can do it all by themselves. But more often, they need help.

Thinking about your dog focuses attention and creates energy. Your thoughts about how much you love him are powerful, and karmic, and karma changes constantly, with every thought and every action.

Now that you've set your intention, spend a few minutes each day just sitting quietly and thinking about your dog. I'm talking about minutes, not hours. Ten minutes is enough. So find a quiet place where you can be alone, turn off your cell phone and get far away from things that beep, blink, vibrate, and tweet. Close your eyes and take a few deep breaths. Think about your dog. Remember him. Love him. Let yourself cry, if you need to cry. Grief can be a kind of purification, stripping away old habits and responses and leaving you sensitive and open to future possibilities.

You're not trying to make anything happen. You're just sitting. So don't judge yourself, or your feelings. Don't intellectualize. Just sit quietly, and wait. Chinese Taoists say, Close your eyes and you will see. Stop listening and you will hear.

Your experience won't necessarily be like mine. But the knowledge you need is out there, and if you can let go of preconceptions and doubt, you'll recognize it when it comes.

This is how you begin. You set your intention, and then you think about your dog. Do this every day. Eventually, something will happen. It may happen while you're sitting and thinking, or a thought may suddenly pop unbidden into your mind while you're doing something else. When it whispers to you, don't discount it or reject it as being wishful thinking or something you imagined.

You may find yourself thinking you should go look into volunteering at a dog shelter, or attend a pet adoption event – not to get another dog, just to look. Or that you should go someplace you don't usually go, or contact someone you haven't heard from in a while. You may even think your dog is somehow trying to "tell you something."

If your dog was lost, you'd look for him. You'd walk around and call his name. In a way, that's what you're doing – although you're doing it with your soul, rather than with your voice. The important thing is to give yourself time and space. Allow yourself to truly listen and the message – or the signal – will eventually become strong enough for you to hear it.

Stop reading. Close this book, and put it away. Find a quiet place, sit down and shut your eyes. There is no better time to start than now.

CHAPTER 2

It takes me nearly six hours to drive as far as Farmington, and I break the trip there, stopping for the night at a motel. I bring Bao's harness and leash and water dish into the motel room with me, just as I would do if he was alive. I hang his leash and harness on a door knob, as I always do, and fill his dish with water and set it down near the bed. I do those things because I can feel he is still with me, and I want him to know that I know he is here.

I am shattered, utterly heartbroken. Everything hurts. I haven't eaten all day, but I'm not hungry. There's a strip mall adjacent to the motel, and I walk across and buy a cheeseburger, but I can't eat it. Just the sight of food makes me feel sick. I sit on the bed, staring sightlessly out the window at nothing. I want to die, and I can't even do that because Bao is already on his way back to me and I have to be here for him. At this point I have no idea about how he'll look, no picture in my mind, nothing like that. I just know he is coming back.

There's a Bible on the nightstand next to my bed. You still find Bibles in most hotel and motel rooms. I know many people who believe that everything in the Bible is the literal truth. When the late Pope Paul II warned the faithful that the devil was still among us, he wasn't speaking allegorically. Catholic Popes – and Catholics all over the world – still believe in the devil, as do 57% of Americans, including U.S. Supreme Court Judge Antonin Scalia.

What does the Bible say about reincarnation? I don't know, and I can't remember. Besides, it doesn't matter. I don't believe in the devil but I don't believe in God, either – not the god of Judaism, Christianity and Islam, at any rate. Maybe that's why this has happened. Maybe God is punishing me. Tears roll down my cheeks. They taste like salt. I tell myself to stop being ridiculous, and put the Bible back into its drawer.

Is Bao really coming back to me? Is such a thing possible? Or am I merely "bargaining" to shield myself from the agonizing pain of bereavement? If I am, I think wryly, it isn't much of a bargain. I can't imagine being more miserable.

Farmington. A long drive. I still have a sense of Bao's presence, as if he's lingering, concerned. This time last night, I was celebrating. I thought we were going to make it. I can't believe he's gone. He was the best thing in my life, the best thing about my life. My only comfort is that it was quick, and that I was spared the euthanasia decision, which is the only thing I can think of that would have been worse than this. And if his disease truly was as bad as they think (and they won't know that until the tests come back) he would eventually have drowned in his own fluids, which is an awful death. But I feel as if a big chunk of my heart has been torn away.

Bao is next to me in bed, all night. I can feel him, curled against the base of my spine, where he always sleeps. And I am comforted. He isn't there, of course. I know that. And yet, he is.

The remainder of the journey is uneventful. Once again, I'm alone in the silence of the moving car. Once again, hours pass. I might as well be in another universe, another dimension. I feel suspended in time and space, surrounded by time and space, alone with my sorrow and my thoughts. There are no distractions. There is only the vast stillness and my own overwhelming grief.

I pass through the Navajo Reservation and pick up I-40 at Gallup, heading west past the Petrified Forest and the sepia-colored towns of Holbrook and Winslow to Flagstaff, then south to Scottsdale. The harsh glare makes everything look one dimensional, as if I'm driving through an old John Ford movie set. Bao is still here, still curled up on the seat beside me.

But he isn't, not in the sense that he was with me two days ago. Bao is gone. There is no getting around that. I'd held his dear, lifeless little body in my arms. I'd felt him slowly grow cold. Thinking about it and reliving those terrible hours fill me with utter desolation. Pulling over to the side of the road, I stop the car, rest my head on the steering and sob.

Afterwards I just sit there for a while staring out at the desert, still feeling Bao's psychic presence. Bao and I had always had a strong karmic connection. When you have that kind of connection with another sentient being – a person or an animal – it usually indicates that you have unfinished business from a previous lifetime. It means there are things you must do to or for one another and things you must learn from one another. Even though Bao is no longer here physically, our karmic connection has survived, allowing his soul to reach out and touch mine. There are still things we need to do together, still things we need to learn.

Coming back to my silent, empty condo cluttered with Bao's toys, my refrigerator filled with Bao's food, the cupboard where I kept his medicines, his two water bowls, one in the kitchen and one in the bedroom, both still filled with water – is horrible beyond describing.

Everything reminds me of Bao. And he is gone. I am overcome with grief. How can I bear to continue live in this place that is so filled with memories? I lay down on the unmade bed and pull the quilt over my head and cry myself to sleep.

The next morning I have to face the awful task of responding to the numerous messages that have been left on my answering machine, telling friends and acquaintances – one by one – that Bao is gone. Everyone is shocked. Everyone says how sorry they are. What else can they say? What can anyone say?

I plod sadly through the hours, preparing meals I don't want, rinsing the dishes and putting them in the dishwasher, collecting the mail and paying the bills. Bao's psychic presence still remains strong, as does my certainty that he is coming back to me. But as strange as it may sound, it doesn't matter. Nothing matters. I am surrounded by pain, suffocated by pain, breathless with pain. I can't imagine how it once felt, not to be in this constant, unrelenting pain.

Jeannie calls me every morning, to see how I'm doing, to tell me about a television movie I might like, to suggest we meet for lunch as soon as I feel up to it. But there is really nothing she can say or do to help. Bao is gone. I loved him more than life itself, and he's gone.

One afternoon – to my utter amazement – I tell a neighbor that Bao is going to reincarnate and come back to me. I just blurt it out. The poor woman murmurs something about being sorry, and hurries away. I'm as surprised as she is. I barely know her.

I stand there, watching her go and wondering what possessed me to say such a thing to a virtual stranger. And why did she say she was sorry? What was she sorry about? That I'd said such a crazy thing out loud? So what if I had? I'm not sorry, I think defiantly. I'm not a bit sorry. I'm glad I said it. It felt good to say it out loud.

When we speak we send tiny pulses of resonating energy into the universe, the way a pebble dropped into a pond creates concentric circles of ripples. The energy can be positive or negative, but either way, it's energy. And energy creates change.

The so-called power of positive thinking recognizes this invisible energy. Thinking really can make it so. Sports psychologists call it visualization, and train athletes to mentally play shots over and over again, imagining the perfect stroke, the perfect serve. Business guru and syndicated columnist Harvey Mackay says, "Fantasizing and projecting yourself into successful situations is one of the most powerful means there is to achieve personal goals." But you don't have to be an athlete or an executive to benefit from positive thinking. When quadriplegics envision themselves in yoga poses, their brain waves become identical to those of people who are actually performing yoga.

If we're all constantly sending energy into the universe, it follows that the universe itself must be in a continual state of flux and that everything must somehow be connected to everything else. Quantum physicists agree. They assure us that the quantum state of every particle in the universe affects the wave function of every other particle, making the entire universe a continuous wave function in which everything is connected.

Physicists call this entanglement. Einstein called it *spukhafte Fernwirkung*, spooky action at a distance. Indian philosophers call it karma, a Sanskrit word that describes the process whereby virtuous actions of body, speech and mind result in happiness and non-virtuous actions of body, speech and mind result in suffering.

Karma is what happens, the result – or ripening – of a previous action. Everything we think, say and do produces karma. Every sentient being creates karma, and all of these karmas continually interact with one another in this life and the next one and even the one after that. The fact that I'm writing these words is affecting my karma. The fact that you are reading them is affecting yours. And because everything is constantly changing, anything is possible.

I don't think positive thinking will bring Bao back to life. Bao is physically dead, and I know that all the positive thinking in the world isn't going to change that. The past is the past. However, the future is pure potentiality, where anything is possible. I still feel Bao's psychic presence. Moreover, I've noticed that every time I think about him or talk about him my awareness of his presence becomes stronger.

Remember the scene in *Peter Pan* where Tinker belle is dying? Peter turns to the audience and begs us to save Tinker belle's life saying, Clap your hands if you believe in fairies! And of course, everyone claps. Belief is important. Belief makes things happen. We are all part of the process. Things don't simply happen to us; they also happen because of us.

Through the rest of that day I make it a point to consciously pause and take time to tell myself that Bao is going to reincarnate. I say the words as if I am repeating a mantra, knowing that each time I utter them, I am sending their energy into the universe. I can feel it. *Bao is coming back to me. Bao is coming back to me. Bao is coming back to me.*

This sounds weird, I know. At the time, I thought it was weird, too. But it seemed to be working, and that was enough for me. I realize that this isn't about rationality. It's about belief, and belief – by definition – isn't rational.

One thing I do know is that I need to keep talking, to tell other people what I'd told my startled neighbor. I especially want to tell Jeannie, although I'm not sure she'll understand. Maybe she'll think I've totally lost it. And maybe she's be right. None of this makes sense. It doesn't matter, though. I have to tell her.

We're very different, Jeannie and I. While I'd studied philosophy and political science and languages in school, Jeannie had been drawn to the hard sciences. If she'd been a boy she'd have probably gone to medical school and become a doctor, like her dad. After majoring in chemistry and zoology, she went on to do graduate work in microbiology, interning as a medical technologist before being recruited by the sales department of a major drug company. Jeannie – it goes without saying – does not have the kind of background conducive to beliefs in ghosts, miracles, or little green men. Or reincarnation.

On the other hand, she's always ready to listen to what other people have to say. She may not agree with you, but she'll always listen. "Just because I don't believe in reincarnation doesn't mean it doesn't exist," Jeannie says. "It just means I don't believe in it. The important thing is that I can't stand seeing you so miserable. If believing Bao is going to reincarnate and come back to you is going to get you through this, then you go right ahead and believe it, girl friend. For all I know, you might be right. I just want you to feel better."

But I don't feel better. After I talk to Jeannie I curl up on the couch, and press Bao's little leather harness to my lips. At that moment I feel very close to him, absolutely certain that he is on his way back to me. I think about Jeannie's belief in science and in the things science has "proven" to be true. I think about the way scientists use the scientific method to replicate results by duplicating all the variables, and repeating the experiments again and again. Science is great, but it has its limitations. How do you replicate something like a gut feeling? How do you prove a belief?

The next day, Dr. Lana telephones from Colorado. The preliminary biopsy results have come back. It was cancer, a rare, aggressive and horrible cancer. Even if Bao had survived the surgery, he might only have had weeks left and they mightn't have been good weeks. In the end – which according to Dr. Lana would have come sooner rather than later – I would have most likely have had to make the final decision. That would have truly destroyed me. It is the only thing I can think of that would have been worse than what had actually happened.

Everything hurts. It is a world of pain. Bao, my dear little boy. I love you. I love you. More and more I feel that somehow he'll come back to me, he'll be reborn in the animal realm, he'll choose that, even though he belongs in a higher realm. He'll choose that, so he can be with me. I miss him. I miss his dear little face, I miss his steadfast presence at my side. Believing that he'll come back to me is irrational, yet I believe in the power of karma, and in the karmic connection Bao and I shared. And I also feel somehow close to him, not so much as a physical presence (as it was during the first few days) but a spiritual presence, something inchoate telling me he is not here in the material world but in another world, another dimension, yet nonetheless with me.

Even as I continue to grieve I know I need to keep on doing whatever strengthens the psychic link between me and Bao. Saying that he is coming back to me – saying it out loud, to other people – seems to be working rather well. But I can't just wander around Scottsdale, accosting strangers and telling them my dog is going to reincarnate.

I live in a huge condominium complex, and inevitably, people ask about Bao. They aren't friends, they're just people who've seen us out walking. When I tell them he's gone, most simply murmur a few polite words and leave it at that. A few are more sympathetic, wanting to know what happened, engaging me in conversation. These are the people I tell.

More often than you'd think – certainly more often than I would have thought – the response is positive and sympathetic. I discover that quite a few other people believe in reincarnation. They don't go around talking about it, but they believe in it. One afternoon, I meet a woman from Chicago whose cat reincarnated. She's an attorney. "I was like you," she says. "I knew he'd come back to me. I just knew. I kept going to the pound, looking for him. And one day, there he was."

But I soon run out of people. It is June, and ferociously hot. Winters in southern Arizona are delightful, but summers are another story. Unless you're a snake or a lizard, you don't really want to be here during the summer. The snowbirds fly home, and everyone else heads for the mountains, or the beach. Scottsdale is a ghost town. It's too hot to go for walks, so I stay indoors with the air conditioning. Some days, I don't talk to anybody except Jeannie.

I decide that if I can't talk about it, I'll write about it. Ever since I was a teenager I've kept journals. Now, I write about what I feel, about grief and loss and love, about my certainty that Bao is coming back to me. I do this several times a day. It feels right, just as talking about him felt right.

If nothing else, writing is cathartic. But that's not why I continue to do it. Writing is another way of sending these pulses of positive energy into the universe. With every sentence, I'm confirming my belief in what I feel and know, strengthening the forces that are bringing Bao back to me. Writing it down is making it happen.

However, writing can also be baffling and frustrating. The words don't always flow. I find it impossible to explain precisely what is happening to me, and how it feels. All these things I sense so strongly and know even though I can't possibly know them defy reification. There seem to be no words to adequately describe what I am experiencing. No matter how many pages I fill, I can't quite explain myself to myself.

"Words or language, as they are written or spoken, do not seem to play any role in my mechanism of thought," writes Albert Einstein. "For me it is not dubious that our thinking goes on for the most part without use of words."

But for me it is very dubious. Knowing something and yet not having the words to explain how or why I know it is unlike anything I have ever experienced. It makes me uncomfortable. On the other hand, the more I write the more firmly I believe in the validity of my feelings, even if I can't describe them. Whatever this is, and however difficult it is to pin it down, it **is** real and it **is** happening

Someone once defined a state of grace as being like a gentle wind moving among fallen leaves, shifting them around to make room for other things, letting the light and air come through. I believe the shock of Bao's death coupled with my long, solitary drive back to Scottsdale brought me into a state of grace that made it possible for me to listen to the universe in a way I had never listened before. Perhaps this is the way we listen to the universe when we are children, before we learn language. I don't know, and I'm not going to try to explain it, because I can't. What I do know is that grief and solitude somehow opened a channel of communication that allowed the psychic link that had always existed between me and Bao to not only survive his death but to actually grow stronger.

When I read back over the thousands of words I wrote during the weeks following Bao's death I rediscover that numinous sense of wider worlds, of a universe full of potentiality. That's how I know this isn't something I imagined, or dreamed. The words are there on the page. No matter what anyone says and no matter how vehemently psychologists may disagree, all of this really **did** happen exactly as I'm describing it. My certainty that Bao was coming back to me wasn't a delusion or a defense mechanism. It was as real as I am.

HOW TO HELP YOUR DOG
REINCARNATE: WEEK TWO

You've set your intention. You've opened your mind to the idea that your dog can reincarnate. You're learning how to sit quietly, how to listen. These are all good, positive things. You're off to a good start.

Have you told anyone what you're doing? Maybe not, perhaps because you're worried about what they'll think. That's okay. Don't talk about it until it feels right to talk about it. You certainly don't want to get into an argument about reincarnation. Arguing creates negative energy. And in any case, it is impossible to argue about a belief.

So instead of talking about it, write about it. Start a journal. It doesn't have to be anything fancy, although it does need to be more than just a few sheets of paper, because your journal is a a concrete symbol of your intent. A spiral bound notebook will do, although you might want to paste a photograph of your dog on the cover, or decorate it in some other, special way.

What should you write? Begin by picturing your dog in your mind's eye. Remember all the things that made him special, all the good times you had together, all the reasons why you love him. These are the things you need to write about. Writing about them sends positive energy into the universe. Next, try to imagine how you'll feel when your dog comes back to you. Try to visualize it. Remember, visualization is not prayer. You are not asking God for anything. You are simply imagining what it will be like to be reunited with your dog, and writing it down. Be positive. Start each sentence with words like, When my dog comes back to me ....

Another day, try writing to your dog the way you'd write a letter. Tell him what's happening. Is it a good day for a walk? Did you cook steak last night, and think about how much he'd like the bone?

You can also use these pages to record your feelings. Describe the thoughts that go through your mind as you sit and remember your dog. Be honest, but try to be positive, too. Remember that every thought you think and every word you write sends a little pulse of energy into the universe. You want that energy to be good energy.

Try to write something every day, even if it is only a sentence or two. If writing doesn't come easily to you, a sentence or two is enough. Don't force it. What matters isn't the number of words you write, but the feeling with which you write them.

Maybe you'll have a set time for writing, or maybe you'll write whenever the spirit moves you. But as time passes, you'll probably find yourself writing more and more. This is not anything like what used to be called "automatic writing" but automatic writing sometimes happens. When you read over what you've written, pay attention to writing that doesn't seem to look like yours – those passages may be important.

Pay attention to your thoughts, too. Especially pay attention to fleeting, odd thoughts. These can come at any time. You may suddenly "see" your dog, or think you hear him bark. This isn't just your imagination, or wishful thinking. It is a tiny morsel of psychic truth. Acknowledge it and accept it, without worrying about what it means.

You are trying to help your dog come back to you, in this life. Many people just like you have been reunited with dogs and other animal companions, so what you're attempting is not hopeless, or impossible. On the other hand, you are not conducting an experiment. You're not trying to prove anything. You don't need to prove anything. This is not about proof. This is about belief.

Accept what comes. Be positive, and have faith in yourself and in what you're doing. The Dalai Lama writes: "Do not give up. If you are pessimistic from the beginning, you cannot possibly succeed. If you are hopeful and determined, you will always find some measure of success. Winning the gold medal does not matter. You will have tried your best."

So don't be impatient with yourself or with the process. You may get results immediately. Or it may take longer. It takes many drops of water to fill a bucket, and many buckets full of water to fill an ocean. Dr. Martin Luther King, Jr. said: "Take the first step in faith. You don't have to see the whole staircase, just take the first step."

CHAPTER 3

In the beginning, grief numbs you. You know what has happened. You know you've suffered a terrible loss. But you keep going, almost as if you're on automatic pilot, talking to people, brushing your teeth, doing what needs to be done. This numbness lasts for several days, but it wears off. And that's when it hits you, a tsunami of anguish and unbearable pain. And nothing helps. Absolutely nothing.

When his dog Buster died, English writer, broadcaster and former Labour deputy leader Lord Hattersley wrote. "I sat in the first floor room in which I work, watching my neighbors go about their lives, amazed and furious that they were behaving as if it was a normal day. Stop all the clocks. Buster was dead."

That's how I feel. Stop all the clocks. Bao is dead.

There are people who say the death of an animal is less traumatic than the death of a human being. But love is love, and when you lose what you love more than anything else in the world, that loss is devastating. Many of us love animals more than we love people. Kathy Rudy, who teaches ethics at Duke University writes, "It would not be an overstatement to say that most of the important and successful relationships I've had in my life have been with nonhuman animals."

And dogs are special. Their relationship with us is unique. Dogs are the only animals that look directly into our eyes, the way we look into the eyes of one another. Dogs are also the only animals who can live with human beings without being tamed by them, and yet continue to breed with their own kind. DNA evidence indicates dogs separated from wolves and became part of our human pack about 100,000 years ago. They've been beside us ever since. Did human beings domesticate dogs? Or did dogs domesticate human beings? According to the latest anthropological studies, this is a moot question. The evidence suggests we co-evolved.

What we do know is that dogs have been with us from the start, long before we settled down in caves, even before the last Ice Age. Throughout that long ordeal of cold and darkness, dogs and humans huddled together for warmth while the mammoth, the giant sloth, the dire wolf, the saber-toothed tiger and hundreds of other species perished in the unforgiving cold. And when the great sheets of ice finally began to recede, we were still there, and we were still together. Perhaps neither humans nor dogs would have made it alone. But we did make it. We survived, and so did our dogs.

"Until one has loved an animal," writes Anatole France, "a part of one's soul remains unawakened."

Condolence cards begin to arrive, containing thoughtful and beautiful words of consolation. I still treasure those cards, and feel immense gratitude towards all the people who went to the trouble to find just the right sentiment. I'm equally grateful to those who made donations to animal charities in Bao's memory.

Jeannie makes a point of talking to me every day, but remains utterly at a loss as to what she can say or do to make me feel better. It isn't that she doesn't understand. Jeannie had been through this heartbreaking loss herself. One of her dogs was poisoned and died as she raced through the night to find a veterinarian. And Jeannie loved her Saber as much as I loved Bao. Jeannie loves all her dogs. But Jeannie is a positive, active person and sitting around brooding isn't her thing. When there's a problem, Jeannie deals with it. When something is broken, she fixes it. When she loses a dog, she buries it in a little cemetery behind her house and goes out and gets another one. That's what she thinks I should do, too. Not right away. But when I'm ready.

I'm not ready. Besides, I don't want another dog. I want Bao. And he's coming back to me. He's already on his way.

Jeannie doesn't argue the point, even though we both know she doesn't believe in reincarnation. We agree to disagree, and leave it at that. The important thing is that she's here for me.

One morning she starts telling me about one of her friends at the gym who's a psychologist and does grief counseling. A really nice woman, Jeannie says. Younger than us, but very intelligent, very caring. Let me give you her number. Maybe you can go and talk to her, just to see if it makes you feel any better.

I'd had counseling after Rollyn died, and I know from experience that it sometimes helps, just having someone to talk to. But the whole idea of grief counseling is to persuade you to accept your loss and move forward, and that's the problem. I don't accept my loss. Bao's psychic presence is precious to me, and it's all I've got. I don't want to let go of it.

All my life, I've been reading accounts of other people's spiritual and psychic experiences. All my life, I've wished that something like that would happen to me. Now it has. It may not be the spiritual experience I would have chosen, but that now it has finally come, I want to embrace it. I certainly don't want to be talked out of it by some psychologist.

"But look at you! You're so miserable! It breaks my heart to see you like this. If you don't want to talk to a psychologist, fine. What about a support group? Aren't there support groups for people when their dog dies?"

Pet loss support groups, they're called. But their goal is the same as grief counseling – to help you work through the grief process and reach acceptance. If there's a support group for people who know their dog is going to reincarnate, I'll join it in a heartbeat. But there isn't any such group. Or if there is, I can't find it.

Driving back from Colorado several days earlier, I had not questioned my intuition. I'd listened – not with my ears, but with every cell of my being – and accepted what came to me. Yielding to the universe, I became part of the universe. But now that I am out of the hermetically sealed silence of my car and back in what we call the real world, those moments of clarity are becoming more difficult to sustain. It is almost like waking up from a dream. I have to go out and buy food. I have to pay the bills. I have to wash the dishes, and my clothes. I have to get the car serviced. I have to answer the telephone. It feels as if I'm losing the ability to listen. I am beginning to question my feelings, and worse, to doubt them.

I still believe Bao is going to reincarnate. His psychic presence remains very strong, especially when I first wake up in the morning. During those early morning moments, feeling him close to me, I am comforted. But the feeling doesn't last. And in any case, it's not the same as having him here, beside me.

As the day wears on, the hours grow longer. There is nothing I need to do, nobody who needs me. I sit in my condo, drink red wine and cry. Life without Bao is unthinkable, and unbearable. Every room is full of memories. We were always together, we always went everywhere together. How am I meant to do this? How can I possibly live without him?

I am in a downward spiral and one hot, bright afternoon five days after Bao's death, I hit bottom. Nothing matters. It suddenly all seems so crazy, so utterly hopeless. When I look into the bathroom mirror a heartbroken, half-crazy, pathetic old woman stares back at me.

I can't do this any more. If I had a gun, I'd shoot myself. If I had pills, I'd take them. But I haven't got a gun, or pills. I go into the living-room. My computer is open on the table. I sit down in front of it and type "dog reincarnation" into the search engine.

I get five million hits.

There are references to dogs that have (or haven't) reincarnated in dozens of articles. There are personal accounts posted in online forums about pets and online pet support groups. There are blogs about dogs. There are hundreds of websites put up by pet psychics and animal communicators who offer to help find lost pets and "connect" with dead ones. I surf from one site to the next, fascinated. Other people loved their dogs as much as I loved Bao. Other people mourned their dogs, just as I was mourning Bao. Other people believe their dogs will reincarnated, just as I believe that Bao would reincarnate. And many of them have done just that.

Not everybody believes in reincarnation. Most of the nonbelievers turn up in discussion threads that have been started by someone whose dog has died, and they tend to be dismissive and scornful rather than persuasive. There is also a lot of nonsense, including a quiz that tells you what kind of dog you'll be in your next life.

One of the things that strikes me is that most of the people who post descriptions of how their dog or cat has reincarnated are women. Most of the pet psychics and animal communicators are women, too. On the other hand, most of the people debunking these stories – and the very idea of reincarnation – are men.

I read through dozens of postings about dogs and cats and birds and horses and even a ferret who have reincarnated and returned to former owners. Quite a few of these accounts are disjointed and full of repetitions and misspellings, the work of individuals who are clearly unaccustomed to expressing themselves in writing. Yet it is these accounts that I find the most moving and convincing. You feel that these people have had to struggle with every word, but are so convinced that what has happened to them is wonderful and so important that the story has to be told, no matter how difficult it is for them to tell it.

I'm convinced that every single one of these people is absolutely certain that the animal they loved and lost has reincarnated and come back to them. I don't think any of them are making it up. Why should they? Why would anyone go to all the time and effort to write such things and post them on the internet if they weren't true? (I don't mean true in the scientific sense, but true in the sense that the people who write them believe they are true) What would be the point of inventing such painstakingly detailed accounts of things that hadn't happened?

None of these pet owners seem to have any philosophical knowledge of Hinduism or Buddhism. They make no effort to explain what has happened to them, or to justify their belief in reincarnation. They simply know that their dog died, and then somehow, often through a series of amazing coincidences, came back to them.

Besides being overwhelmingly female, the authors have other things in common. All of them describe being utterly devastated by the death of their dog. Many describe experiencing the same kind of psychic presence that I'm observing. All of them describe a process of mourning that continues for weeks, sometimes even years. All of them find themselves constantly thinking of their dog, even dreaming about him. Many also describe an inability to dispose of the dog's toys, or bedding, or collar.

Some of them seek help from a pet psychic and their accounts tell of a detailed and explicit process of consciously searching for – and ultimately finding – their dog. But many others do nothing of the kind. They are somehow guided to a place or an event – and there he is! The dog knows them, and they know their dog. When they bring him home, he knows where his water dish is. He recognizes his toys. At night, he happily curls up just where he always used to sleep. It's the same story, again and again.

I've heard of pet psychics, but I never dreamed there were so many of them. And not just pet psychics – animal communicators and medical intuitives, as well. All of these people (again, mostly women) claim to be able to communicate directly with your dog and tell you what he is feeling and thinking. They don't need to meet your dog in person. Some of them don't even need a photo. You just tell them your dog's name and they're usually able to "tune in" to him. Of course, the dog has to be willing to communicate. This is why it is so difficult for pet psychics and pet communicators to find lost dogs. Often, they tell us, lost dogs want to stay lost.

There doesn't seem to be a lot of difference between pet psychics, animal intuitives and animal communicators, although different individuals offer different services. Some simply offer to communicate with your dog. Others run classes to teach you how to communicate with your pet yourself. And a few specialize in finding lost or missing animals.

Brent Atwater, Medical Intuitive, Animal Reincarnation Authority and founder of something called The Global Pet Loss Hope Initiative does it all. She hosts podcasts, runs classes and offers private consultations. She's also written several books about her dog Friend – who reincarnated and came back to her on no less than five separate occasions – lengthy excerpts of which are posted on her various websites.

According to Atwater (and other pet psychics) every living being vibrates at a certain frequency, and these vibrations are as individual and unique as fingerprints or snowflakes. So it literally is a question of being able to tune in, and some people – like Atwater – seem to be born with the ability to do this.

5000 years ago Vedic philosophers determined that the universe vibrates, and identified 108 separate frequencies. Modern theoretical physicists agree. Our universe – and everything in it – vibrates. The smallest constituents of matter are thought to be tiny, one-dimensional "strings" of energy which vibrate at different frequencies, creating a background hum pitched many times lower than human hearing.

So when pet psychics or animal communicators talk about tuning in to the subtle energy that pervades the universe, it is a reasonably accurate description. The term "subtle energy" refers to the invisible, indestructible vibrations that animate our both our physical bodies and our "subtle bodies". This is sometimes called the universal life force, or bioenergy. It transcends time and space, and permeates everything in the universe. You might say it is what causes the vibrations. No matter what name you give to these vibrations, their existence forms the basis for many ancient and modern medical interventions, including acupuncture, acupressure, bioenergetics, polarity therapy, reflexology, reiki and therapeutic touch.

You can't see bioenergy, or hear vibrations that are below the human threshold of sound, or photograph the subtle body. You can't measure such phenomena. They do not readily lend themselves to scientific analysis. But that's okay. We accept many things we don't understand, from why aspirin works to Einstein's theory of relativity. Einstein suggested that our notions of time, space and mass were relative – rather than absolute – and actually coexist as a four-dimensional continuum. It was Einstein who came up with The Twins Paradox. If one twin gets on a space ship that travels at almost the speed of light and travels to a star twenty light-years away, when he returns to earth his twin will be twenty years older than he is. Reality itself is relative. "Logic will get you from A to B," said Einstein. "Imagination will take you everywhere.

What all this means is that consciousness – with all the thoughts and feelings that encompass it – is ultimately vibration, produced by complex chemical and electrical change that continually takes place in the brain. Imaginative neuroscientists have harnessed thought vibrations and used them to power machines that follow simple "thought" commands. The implications for medicine – the most scientific of sciences – are momentous. Neurosurgeon Dr. C. Norman Shealy writes: "To be truly effective, the practice of healing in the future must merge traditional medicine with a deeper understanding of the human energy system."

But you don't have to be a neurosurgeon or a psychic to harness thought vibrations. Hammacher Schlemmer's "Mind Controlled UFO" is described as a device that "uses your focussed brain waves to remotely control its flight ... using theta wave activity produced by your brain." The Mind Controlled UFO is not a scientific instrument. It's a toy, albeit an expensive one, with a price tag of $229.95

So far, so good. Bioenergy resides in the body. Vibrations emanate from the body. But when the body is gone, what happens to the bioenergy and the vibrations? What am I to make of pet psychics who claim to be able to communicate with dogs and cats who are already dead? Does consciousness require a brain? Or are our brains merely an interface between our immortal, indestructible souls and our bodies?

If what we call the soul is ultimately energy, and indestructible, why shouldn't psychics be able to connect with the souls of departed human beings – or for that matter with animals?

It surprises me to learn that many pet psychics and animal communicators come out of more or less conventional scientific backgrounds. Former wildlife biologist and environmental scientist Marta Williams writes:

"I didn't start out in this field believing that animals could reincarnate and come back to you in a different body, but after years of talking with animals and hearing people's experiences, I now believe this to be the case. I know many people find this hard to accept, or it is contrary to their beliefs. I am not trying to convince anyone, but merely presenting what I now believe to be true about life after death.

"I believe that our animals love being with us, and that they come back to be with us over and over in this lifetime and in future lifetimes. I also believe that they find their way to us; we don't have to do much except to pay attention and react appropriately when we sense that there is some unusual connection or situation with an animal that we encounter. When my animals die, I tell them that I would love to have them back and ask them to please find me and make it obvious to me if and when they return. It is their decision. Then I let go and wait to see what happens.

"I am still waiting for Dougal, my chocolate wolf-hound, to come back. I got a strong sense from him that he wanted to be a very tiny dog in his next life. It has been a few years since he died, and nothing has happened yet, But I am being careful not to rush it. Dougal will come back if and when he is ready, and he will find me and make it obvious, of that I am sure. Maybe I will find a little dog abandoned in the road, or a friend will call and say they have a little dog they can't keep. Somehow, I am sure Dougal will be with me again."

The idea of Dougal wanting to be a small dog in his next life makes me smile. Many dogs apparently do have specific ideas as to who and what they will be in their next life. Big dogs sometimes want to be small dogs, and vice versa. Some dogs want to be the same breed as they were in their former lives, but others want to try something different. A Maltese might want to be a Pit Bull. An Australian Sheep Dog might want to be a Chihuahua. A white dog might want to be black. Bao had been a beautiful dog, and he knew he was beautiful, and he loved being beautiful. I suspect that he wants to be beautiful again, and that's why he's coming back as a Shih Tzu.

No matter what their background, pet psychics and animal communicators insist there is nothing magical about what they do. Many of them believe that all of us are capable of communicating with animals, that this is a natural ability that we've somehow lost along the way to modernity. I was struck by the matter-of-fact tone of most of this material. There was nothing mysterious or mystical about communicating with animals, according to these people.

One of the many people author Arthur Myers interviewed for his insightful book about aniaml communication is clairvoyant and animal diagnostician Nancy Regalmuto. She explains: "We can all do it, these are divine rights. We're all coming from the same Creator, the same place. We're all the same essentially in our makeup, we all have the same abilities, the same rights. But a lot of people have given up their rights. They don't even know what their rights are. You have a right to be able to communicate with all things that God created. This is our divine right. A lot of people think, You can do it, Nancy, because you're gifted. Well, you're gifted too, it's just tht you don't recognize your gifts. Those gifts are under all our Christmas trees. I just opened mine."

Many animal communicators include testimonials from clients whose pets have reincarnated on their websites. These long and meticulous accounts of dog reincarnation are well-written and – as you'd expect – go into great detail about the kind of assistance the pet psychic has provided. But basically, the story remains the same. Someone mourns and grieves inconsolably for their dog, refusing to believe that he is gone, somehow knowing that he will come back. At the end of each story, with the help and encouragement of the animal psychic, dog and owner are finally reunited.

Most of accounts I read are about dogs who are reborn as puppies and subsequently reunited with their owners. However there are a handful of other versions of the story that initially puzzle me. In these cases, the deceased dog and his grieving owner are reunited almost immediately, often within days or a week or so following the dog's death. How can that be? I'd always thought reincarnation obeyed the laws of nature. Since the gestation period for dogs is about 62 days, how can it be possible for a woman who'd lost her beloved dog on Monday to find him again at the local pound the following Saturday morning?

When this what happens, it isn't – technically – reincarnation. These kinds of events, I learn, are called "walk-ins". The deceased dog's spiritual essence takes possession of another, living dog's body, not by force but by mutual consent. The dead dog wants to resume life in this particular time and place, and the living dog – for whatever reason – is ready to move to a different realm. So they agree to a swap, whereby spirit of the deceased dog literally walks in and takes over the physical body of the dog who is ready to leave.

Apparently, if you're a dog or any other kind of animal, being a walk-in is relatively easy. The trickiest part of the process, I suppose, is for the deceased and newly disembodied dog to find a reasonably young and healthy dog who lives somewhere near his owner and who is willing to consent to the swap. The biggest disadvantage is that the "walk in" dog has no memory of anything that happened to him in his present life up until the moment he walked in. Still, if he can find his owner and resume his former life, it doesn't matter.

I admit that the idea of a "walk-in" is harder for me to accept than simple, straightforward reincarnation. But it does explain reunions of dogs and owners which would otherwise be inexplicable. If I accept the accounts of people who claim their dog reincarnated, then it seems to me I must also accept the accounts of people who manage to find their dog mere days or weeks after his death.

Of course, anyone can write anything and post it on the internet. Just because it's on the internet doesn't make it true. I remind myself that pet psychics and animal communicators are also business people, offering their services in the marketplace and seeking customers for their recordings, books and consultations They aren't hobbyists. They expect to be paid. Their websites are advertisements for their services and should probably, I think, be taken with the proverbial grain of salt.

But what about the dozens of other accounts I've read? What did any of these people have to gain by telling their stories in such detail? If what they are saying isn't true, why would they bother?

This is a whole new world, and I am intrigued. I even consider contacting a pet psychic myself. It isn't all that expensive. And it's easy enough to do. They've all set themselves up with toll free numbers, and informative, recorded messages. No charge, no obligation. You leave your name and number, and they get back to you.

And then what? I already know Bao is coming back to me. So why contact a pet psychic? For verification? For reassurance? But won't that be the same as projecting doubt into the universe? No, I don't want to do that. I already know everything I need to know.

One week after Bao's death, I recite the ritual prayers to help him progress towards a good rebirth. I didn't think he needs them. He is already on his way back to me. He is in his mother's womb, a tiny embryo nestled with his brothers and sisters. Still, prayers never hurt.

HOW TO HELP YOUR DOG
REINCARNATE: WEEK THREE

You're allowing yourself to mourn, and you've been learning how to listen. You're already writing in a journal. Your dog will reincarnate. If you want him to come back to you, he will. But you have to want it. You have to want it so badly that you can imagine it happening.

You may be fortunate enough to have discovered you possess psychic powers you never expected. Maybe you've already found your dog, or have a strong intuition about where and how to look for him.

If not, don't worry. It's still early days.

Either way, you must be prepared for people who will try to talk you out of believing your dog will come back to you. Don't argue with them. Remind yourself that they mean well. They are entitled to their beliefs, just as you are entitled to yours.

If nothing seems to be happening, you may be trying too hard. Remember the old Glen Campbell song, "Gentle On My Mind"? The idea isn't to think about your dog every minute of the day but rather, to continue to live your life with your dog always "gentle on your mind." So don't obsess. Just let go and float with the energy, the way you'd float down a river on a raft.

There's also the possibility that things are happening and you haven't noticed. We're all so "plugged in" these days, bombarded with thousands of verbal and nonverbal messages, filtering out everything we don't "need" to know. So be vigilant.

What you're seeking may arrive as a piece of music playing over and over again in your mind, or an advertising slogan, or an image from a billboard. Psychic messages are often symbolic. Why is this bit of music – or this slogan, or this image – so vivid? What does it evoke?

Nonverbal information is important. We trust it, intuitively. This is why pharmaceutical advertisements show images of happy people playing on the beach with their children or chasing butterflies as a voice-over quietly describes the potentially devastating side-effects of the drug being advertised. We remember the images, not the warnings.

So pay attention to the nonverbal promptings of instinct and intuition, including fleeting thoughts, hunches, and daydreams. These come naturally, if we just allow them to do so. They don't come to you through your eyes and ears, but through your soul. In other times and other cultures, leaders and wise men actively sought such promptings, but we don't. We don't take them seriously. We have forgotten how to listen. Yet with practice, we can learn. We all still have the necessary equipment, even though it's stiff and rusty from centuries of non-use.

Certainly, consider a consultation with an animal communicator or an animal psychic, if this appeals to you. There is a sound, scientific basis for the things these people claim to be able to do, and they've helped many bereaved pet parents reunite with their beloved animal companion.

Provided you have access to a computer, finding them should be easy. But take your time, and be selective. As with any profession, some animal communicators are probably better than others. Choose with your soul, as well as with your mind. Read through the material you find on their web pages, and notice which ones just "feel" right. Go with that feeling, and you probably won't go wrong.

Should you try to find someone local? I don't really think it matters, although some people prefer face to face contact. In any case, your initial contact will probably be by telephone. Again, be aware of how it feels, talking to this person. What kind of vibes are you getting? Remember, it has to feel right because if it doesn't, it probably won't work. And remain open to the idea that perhaps, you don't need an animal communicator.

Finally, don't reject anything because it seems too easy or too obvious. If your dog died more than eighteen weeks ago, he may be someplace nearby, waiting for you. He may be one of a litter of puppies. He may be in a shelter. He may be in a good home, the beloved companion of someone who – for whatever reason – will be forced to give him up. If you feel a sudden urge to check out a local dog adoption event, do it. You may not find your dog there. But you may meet someone who will eventually help you find him. Something will send you towards him. Something will send him towards you. So be ready.

Keep him gentle on your mind, like a strand of seaweed floating upon the tide. Remember, there are no coincidences. Everything happens for a purpose, and the universe is unfolding exactly as it should.

CHAPTER 4

Somehow, a week passes. When I wake up the Friday morning after Bao's death I think, *This time last week Bao was still alive.*

Throughout the day, I remember where we'd been and what we'd been doing at this time last week. The day had begun with our happy little morning walk, Bao prancing along so cheerfully that even with the surgery looming I was able to persuade myself that everything was going to be okay. We'd spent most of the morning at the clinic, Bao sleeping peacefully at my side. Just before noon, I remembered how they'd brought him back to me after he'd had his first sedatives, so that he could wait next to me, rather than in a cage. I'd kissed his dear little nose before they took him to the operating room and whispered, *I love you to the moon and back.*

Bao was in surgery during the slow, sunlit afternoon hours. All I could do is wait. I remember at one point

Dr. Lana came out and ushered me into a small, private room where she explained that it was worse than anyone thought. She said they were doing their best, but the unspoken message was that Bao might not survive. Alone again, I remember how I kept looking at the clock, wishing for it to be over. I remember how frightened I was, how helpless I felt.

Finally, Dr. Lana came out to tell me they were "closing" – he'd made it, after all. Less than an hour later, Bao was awake in the recovery room. He was on his feet, staggering and dopey but making himself comfortable curled up against the stuffed toy I'd brought for him. He always liked to sleep that way, with his head on one of his stuffed animals.

Now, watching the sun sink behind the buildings to the west. I think, This time last week, I was driving back to the motel, dazed and giddy with relief. And grateful, so grateful. And unaware that Bao had less than six hours to live.

But what could we have done differently? His pericardial sac was filling with fluid yet again, the surgery had been his only hope. I knew it then and I know it now. Sitting here in my silent condo, alone with my thoughts, I want to blame someone. But there is nobody to blame. Nobody had done anything wrong. Everyone had done their best.

Buddhists think that after death our consciousness – our spiritual essence – remains in a sort of limbo which is called the bardo of becoming. Sogyal Rinpoche likens it to a transit lounge, where we await the connection to our next life. Our rebirth depends upon how quickly we are able to make a karmic connection with our future parents.

Most beings remain in the bardo of becoming for three weeks before finding their future parents and preparing to reenter the bardo of life. Some take longer. On the other hand, when an individual's karma – good or bad – is very strong, the entire process can take place in a split second.

I think that's how it was with Bao. I think he went straight to his mother's womb. That was why they'd been unable to revive him, when his heart stopped. They couldn't bring him back because he was already someplace else. I lie awake for hours that Friday night, envisioning Bao as a tiny embryo in his mother's womb, snuggled with his brothers and sisters. I can actually see them, in my mind's eye. They look like tiny lima beans.

But when I open my eyes the next morning, all I feel is the searing sorrow of loss. I get up and get dressed, going leadenly through the motions. But there is no respite, no escape from the constant pain. I can't read. I can't work. I can't concentrate. I can't even watch Lifetime movies. All I want is for it to get dark, so that I can crawl back into bed and escape into the oblivion of sleep. But the days are getting longer as we near the summer solstice. and when twilight finally comes, it lingers on and on.

Telephone calls from friends and acquaintances have tapered off except for Jeannie, who makes a point of talking to me at least once a day. I know this isn't because people think Bao was "only" a dog. This is what happens when someone dies. You're allowed to mourn for a few days but that's it. The earth keeps turning. Life, as they say, goes on. I remember this is how it was when my husband died. I remember how hurt and angry I felt.

I am still comforted by Bao's psychic presence, but it's his physical presence that I miss, and mourn, and need. I need my dear little dog, and I wake up each morning, missing him. I will never hold him again. His dear little tongue will never cover my face with kisses. All of that is over, finished. I am wretched.

In addition to my own prayers I've arranged for weekly prayers to be said for Bao at a local Buddhist center. This will continue for seven weeks. It's called phowa, a practice meant to guide the deceased towards a good rebirth.

Maybe you're thinking that my knowing Bao is already on his way back to me should be comforting me. It isn't. Although I know it, I don't believe it. How **can** I believe it? Other people don't believe it. Other people think I've totally lost it. Maybe they're right. I'm a mess.

Jeannie joins the chorus of well-meaning people who think I should begin to consider bringing another dog into my life. She offers to go with me to a pet shop or to see a breeder and look at puppies or even visit the pound, if I want to rescue a dog. "Maybe you're right," Jeannie says. "Maybe Bao is coming back to you. Maybe he's already back, waiting for you to come and get him and bring him home. Shouldn't you be trying to find him?"

"Not yet," I told her. "He isn't in a pet shop, or a shelter. He's an embryo, growing in his mother's womb with his brothers and sisters. I have to wait for him to be born. Probably, it won't be until the beginning of August."

"But that's nearly two months from now! You can't go on like this for another two months! Gail, you're like me. We're dog people. You need a new dog in your life."

What could I say?

I **did** need a new dog in my life, the same way many widows need a new husband. Speaking as someone who has suffered both kinds of loss, I think they're really not all that different. You love your husband, and you love the life you share together. Suddenly, that life is gone. When the first shock of grief wears off, you realize this, and it can be devastating. It's not just your husband that's gone. The entire structure and underpinning of your life is gone as well. I suspect this is why many widows and widowers remarry so quickly. When author Joyce Carol Oates lost her husband, she wrote a book about what it was like to be widowed, but by the time it was published she had already remarried.

Sharing your life with a dog involves the same sort of reciprocal and emotionally satisfying interactions that characterize human relationships. Best Friends Animal Society Publications and Creative Director Elissa Jones writes of life after adopting her "perfect" dog Dulcinea. "I no longer needed to hit the gym for what I considered boring forms of cardio exercise. With Dulcie by my side I took sometimes four walks a day. These walks became a kind of meditation for me, a time when I communed with nature, with Dulcie and with my own thoughts. I found laughter in the very single-minded focus that a dog gives when she wants you to throw the ball, pick up the leash or do just about anything. And perhaps most surprising of all to me, I found a whole new group of friends on a visit to the park in my neighborhood. There, a met a friendly bunch who gathered in a remote corner of the park every night at 5:30. The only thing we had in common was that we all brought with us at least one dog. Talking with people who didn't necessarily share my political beliefs or my alma mater and who didn't even know what I did for a living – but who did share that powerful love of a pet – was a revelation. In those evenings at the park, I found a kind of balance I didn't even know I'd been missing."

If your dog was your sole companion, the pleasure is even more intense. But so is the loss. "When (my dog) died, it didn't merely leave a hole in my single-person household," writes Washington Post journalist Joe Yonan. "It was as if someone had rearranged my life, excising without permission many of the rituals that had governed it." And there are a lot of us like Joe. Over a third of American households are single-person households.

After my Australian friend Christopher lost his Gumnut, he nonetheless continued to take his morning walks in the park, carrying "poop" bags and chatting with the other dog owners, joking that he now had an "invisible" dog. And within weeks, Christopher rescued Will and Grace from the pound, and they're now all living happily ever after.

Bao and I were together for nearly twelve years, enjoying breakfast cuddles, morning and afternoon walks, and all the little games and rituals that gave pleasure to us both. The morning walk in particular had been an integral part of our lives. I miss that morning walk. I miss our joyous morning kisses. I miss our games. I miss the evening ritual of preparing Bao's dinner. Where there had been balance, now there is a gaping void. Bao and I were a couple. Now I am alone.

My friend Lynn telephones from Florida. She's just heard the news. I've known Lynn since we were in grade school. I tell her how strongly I feel that Bao will reincarnate, and come back to me. "I know how crazy it sounds," I add.

"It doesn't sound crazy at all. Bao loved you so much. Of course he'd want to come back to you. Besides, miracles happen."

I think she's just trying to make me feel better. But she's right. Miracles do happen. Every day, events occur that can't be explained by science. Sometimes we call them coincidences. Sometimes we call them luck. We tend not to demand explanations, because we know there are many things we can't explain or understand. So we read our horoscopes and play our lucky numbers. We feel good and bad "vibes" about people, and sometimes places. We experience the curious thing called *deja vu*. We fall in love. We're not really as reasonable as we like to think we are.

Reincarnation is one of the things we don't understand. The idea of reincarnation is as old as mankind. But reincarnation wasn't (as many people seem to think) a story we told one another to stave off our fear of death. In fact, it was just the opposite. Ancient Indian philosophers viewed life – rather than death – as the thing to be feared. Life was suffering. Life was pain. Life was an existential treadmill from which there was no escape, and reincarnation kept the treadmill turning. To be reborn again and again was to be condemned to an eternal cycle of suffering and pain.

The ancient Greeks also believed in reincarnation, although they called it metempsychosis, or the transmigration of the soul. It is said that Pythagoras (who claimed to remember some of his former lives) stopped another man from beating a dog saying: Don't beat it. It is the psyche of a friend of mine - I recognize him by his voice. Many other people who have little or no knowledge of Buddhism believe in reincarnation, as well. Jews believe in reincarnation. Early Christians believed in reincarnation. Henry Ford believed in reincarnation.

For the Indian philosophers, the question was not, How can I reincarnate? but rather, How can I escape reincarnation? Nearly three thousand years ago, Siddharta Gautama offered his followers a way out. Our desires create illusory phenomena, he said. These illusions delude us into believing we have a "self" that experiences them, and it is this "self" that is continually reborn. But once you've freed yourself from desire, you'll realize this "self" does not exist. This is enlightenment. Siddharta Gautama came to be known as Buddha, the Enlightened One.

This is a gross oversimplification of an extremely complicated philosophical system, but the point is that Buddha (who was a real, historical person) and his contemporaries were not seeking eternal life. For these ancient Indian philosophers, reincarnation was not a comforting belief, but an unfortunate fact of existence.

So where's the proof? There isn't any. Proof belongs to science. Reincarnation is belief. And science and belief – in the words of Stephen Jay Gould – occupy "non-overlapping magisteria". Science concerns itself with questions of fact. Belief concerns itself with questions of meaning. By definition, you can't prove a belief. You can only believe it.

While there's no proof of reincarnation, there is an abundance of evidence suggesting that reincarnation – or transmigration of the soul, or rebirth, call it what you will – exists. Admittedly, most of this evidence is what scientists like to call anecdotal, provided by people – most often children – who claim to remember a former life. Interestingly, these memories frequently turn out to be quite accurate. Sogyal Rinpoche offers this example in *The Tibetan Book of Living and Dying:*

"Her name was Kamaljit Kour, and she was the daughter of a schoolteacher in a Sikh family in the Punjab of India. One day, on a visit to a local fair with her father, she suddenly asked him to take her to another village, some distance away. Her father was surprised and asked her why. 'I have nothing here,' she told him. 'This is not my home. Please take me to that village. One of my school-friends and I were riding on our bicycles when suddenly we were hit by a bus. My friend was killed instantly. I was injured in the head, ear and nose. I was taken from the site of the accident and laid on the bench in front of a small courthouse nearby. Then I was taken to the village hospital. My wounds were bleeding profusely and my parents and relatives joined me there. Since there were no facilities to cure me in the local hospital they decided to take me to Ambala. As the doctors said I could not be cured, I asked my relatives to take me home.' Her father was shocked, but when she insisted, he finally agreed to take her to the village ...

"They went to the village ... and she recognized it as they approached, pointing out the place where the bus had hit her, and asking to be put in a rickshaw, whereupon she gave instructions to the driver ... her father, who still did not believe her, asked the neighbors whether there was a family like the one Kamaljit Kour had described, who had lost their daughter. They confirmed the story, and told the girl's astonished father that Rishma, the daughter of the family, had been sixteen years old when she was killed; she had died in the car on the way home from the hospital.

"The father felt extremely unnerved by this, and told Kamaljit that they should go home. But she went right up to the house, asked for her school photo and gazed at it with delight. When Rishma's grandfather and uncles arrived, she recognized and named them without mistake. She pointed out her own room, and showed her father each of the other rooms in the house. Then she asked for her school books, her two silver bangles and her two ribbons, and her new maroon suit. Her aunt explained that these were all things Rishma had owned …

"Kamaljit Kour was born ten months after Rishma died. Although the little girl had not yet started school, she often pretended to read, and she could remember the names of all her school friends in Rishma's school photograph. Kamaljit Kour had also always asked for maroon-colored clothes. Her parents discovered that Rishma had been given a new maroon suit of which she was very proud, but she had never had time to wear it. The last thing Kamaljit Kour remembers of her former life was the lights of the car going out on the way home from the hospital …"

Psychiatrist Dr. Ian Stevenson of the University of Virginia collected over 2500 similar case studies of children who claimed to remember past lives. Some of their bodies bore actual, physical scars they'd received in a previous life. Fourteen of them remembered that they'd been shot to death, and their scars resembled the entry and exit wounds made by bullets. Coincidence? Stevenson didn't think so, and in 1967 he founded the Division of Perceptual Studies within the Department of Psychiatry and Neurobehavioral Sciences at the University of Virginia, currently under the direction of Dr. Jim Tucker. It is one of a dozen such research units around the world.

When we talk about the real world, we're talking about a world we can see, hear, smell, taste and touch. We're talking about a world of matter. But we also know that matter is composed of molecules so tiny that they are invisible to the human eye, and that all these molecules are in fact in constant motion. The real world isn't solid, and unchanging. The real world is constantly in motion.

"... everything solid is transitory; every particle in existence is oscillating in and out of the void, giving the illusion of solidity because our senses aren't quick enough to catch the vibration ... The same is true for you and me. We exist as a fluid product of change and stability. Our brains look the same from moment to moment, but the activity of neurons in never exactly the same – a brain is like a river where one cannot step into the same place twice," Deepak Chopra writes. "If the universe is constantly re-creating itself, we would be the only aspect that isn't involved, which doesn't make sense ... Nature depends on the mechanism of rebirth."

Being reincarnated is not the same as getting your old life back. Death is an ending and when you reincarnate you are born a new being, in a new life. Your past lives and your present life are still connected by karmic links but when you were born into this life, your karma was shuffled and recombined to become the unique entity that is – at the moment – you.

So why don't we remember our former lives? Partly, because of the nature of memory itself. We tend to remember "big" things. Memory is attached to strong emotions, which may be why children who died violent, traumatic deaths in a former life are able to recall them in this one. Certainly, we don't remember everything that happens to us, even in this life. Memory is selective. It has to be. Otherwise, we'd go mad.

Moreover, our Western culture discourages such memories. (They're much more common in India) In the United States, if a child claims to remember a former life his parents are likely to think he's merely "going through a phase" like having imaginary friends.

In any case, these memories soon fade. Most memories fade. Can you remember what you had for lunch last Tuesday? Or who was invited to your seventh birthday party? If we can't remember where we put the car keys, it's no wonder we can't remember our former lives.

All sentient beings reincarnate. Shih Tzus in particular have a long tradition of returning to live out a second life with a beloved owner. It is said that they were specially bred by Tibetan monks to sleep in the sleeves of their gowns and keep them warm while they meditated. Each Shih Tzu traditionally spent two "lifetimes" with his or her monk, who could always tell instantly which puppy in a litter was "his" Shih Tzu by the white blaze (said to have been placed there by Buddha) on its forehead.

Almost a century ago, Edwin Schrodinger asked: "How can the events in space and time which take place within the spatial boundary of a living organism be accounted for by physics and chemistry?"

His conclusion: They can't.

Science can only take us so far.

HOW TO HELP YOUR DOG
REINCARNATE: WEEK FOUR

Deep down inside, you believe your dog can come back to you. You believe this is possible. You believe this can happen, and you also believe that you can help to make it happen. You believe all of these things, and you are right to believe them, because they're true.

You're reading this book because you and your dog shared a special, karmic bond, a bond that still exists, a bond that transcends death.

Thinking about your dog and writing about him is sending pulses of positive energy into the universe. Talking about him will release even more of this powerful, positive energy. I still remember how amazingly good it felt the first time I said, Bao is going to reincarnate. Bao is coming back to me. However, unless you live in a Buddhist community you may find this difficult. You don't want people to think you're crazy. Nor do you want to find yourself in an argument about reincarnation. Arguing is unpleasant, and creates negative vibrations.

So who should you talk to? Perhaps a family member. Perhaps a friend. Perhaps your hairdresser.

If you recently lost your dog, people will often provide the opening you need when they offer their condolences. After you've chatted for a few minutes, guide the conversation in that direction by saying something like, I've been reading this really interesting book by a woman whose dog reincarnated ... and see where it goes from there. If your dog has been gone for a while, start with the people in your life who truly understand how much you miss him. Use the same technique.

Some people will come right out and say they don't believe in reincarnation. Others will shake their heads or roll their eyes. That's fine. Change the subject, and find someone else.

Talking to total strangers can be very effective, too. Sometimes, it's easier to talk to a stranger. If you see someone walking a dog on the street or in a park, approach them and start a conversation. You might say how beautiful their dog is. Or that he reminds you of your dog. One thing will easily lead to the next.

You'll find lots of people who believe in reincarnation, just as I did. They don't talk openly about their beliefs because – like you and me – they're not sure what the reaction will be. So they're not easy to find. But they're definitely out there.

Does the thought of doing these things make you feel uneasy? Then don't do them, because they're not right for you. Always trust your instincts. Always follow your gut. Everyone is different, and techniques that worked for me will not necessarily work for you.

Remember, you need to be sending that positive energy into the universe. How you do it isn't important, so long as you do it. If face to face conversations with friends and neighbors aren't your thing, try exploring some of the many "dog reincarnation" websites and joining – or starting – a discussion thread. A virtual community is still a community, even if you're all using made-up names. Bear in mind that each time you're able to tell someone "I think my dog is going to come back to me" you make the psychic bond that exists between you and your dog just that little bit stronger. It doesn't matter whether that person is standing in front of you, or somewhere in cyberspace. It's your intention and your attention that count.

Continue to write in your journal. Continue to pay attention to your thoughts, and your dreams. Be patient. The bond between you and your dog is a karmic bond. You will find one another. You will be together again.

CHAPTER 5

Even before he made his first million, Warren Buffet says he never doubted for a moment that someday he'd be rich. I wish I could say I never doubted Bao would come back to me. The truth is, doubt can strike at any moment. When it does, it is as bleak and black and overwhelming as an Oklahoma dust storm. Certainty vanishes. Hope vanishes. Doubt is horrible.

Belief can't be rationalized. You either believe, or you don't. Sometimes, I do. Other times, I don't. It might be different if I had a religious background that allowed me to fit my beliefs and doubts into some kind of spiritual matrix. But I don't. Emotionally and spiritually, I am in uncharted waters.

"Where is the boundary between reality and illusion?" asks Michael Roads, author of *Talking To Nature*. "Who decides what is real and what is illusion? Do we accept a common belief or can we have an independent belief, isolated but real? How much of our experience is an illusion, based on what we think is reality?"

The more I struggle with doubt, the worse it gets. Trying to be reasonable doesn't work. Reason just makes it worse. My logical, critical left brain is worse than useless. It stands between me and what I believe, like a dark cloud blotting out the sun.

Neurosurgeon Dr. Eben Alexander suggests that our brain acts as a filter, blocking our access to higher worlds. "We need to accept – at least hypothetically – that the brain itself doesn't produce consciousness. That it is, instead, a kind of reducing valve or filter that dumbs down consciousness for the duration of our human experience."

Yet I continue to try to reason with myself. Fighting doubt just seems to feed it, but I don't know what else to do. I'm like the Tibetan monk who creeps into a cave to meditate only to discover it is filled with demons. He tries to attack the demons. He tries to hide from them. He tries to scare them away. Nothing works. Finally he gives up. If I have to share my cave with demons, he thinks, then I will. And at that point, the demons vanish.

The best way to deal with doubt, writes Andro Mueller Roshi, is "... not indulge it, but go on with it. This is essentially an experience of faith. It is not a feeling, it's a willingness."

It's like finding yourself in a rip when you're swimming in the sea. You can't swim against a rip. It's too strong. So you swim at an angle to the rip, letting it carry you until you swim out of it.

I know in less than two months Bao would be born, in a new body. I know he'll be a Shih Tzu. And I know he'll have a good birth, which means I won't find him in a pet shop or a dog shelter. Find him? This is the first time it has occurred to me that I will need to find him. He'll be a puppy, helpless. How **will** I find him? Where will I even begin?

Finally, my left brain has something to chew on. Obviously, I need to start by contacting people who breed Shih Tzus, and find out which breeders are expecting litters in early August. So what I need is a list. That should be easy enough. But when I sit down in front of the computer, I freeze. Just days ago, Bao was here in this very room, sleeping at my feet as I worked. My eyes fill with tears. I can't do this.

Maybe I don't have to. Maybe I'll just find him. Maybe I'll hear about a litter of puppies and go to see them, and there he'll be. But suppose I find him, only to discover that he's already been sold? It's not uncommon for people to "reserve" a pedigreed puppy in advance, and the first person to put down a deposit usually gets pick of the litter. That's what Rollyn and I did years ago, when we bought Rosie. No, I need to find him. I need to start looking for him now.

I switch on the computer. I'm not looking for a puppy, I remind myself. I'm only looking for a list of breeders. However, my initial searches yield thousands of websites offering general information about Shih Tzus, dog trainers, pet supply companies, on-line veterinarians, Shih Tzu themed calendars, license plates and T-shirts, blogs and Shih Tzu breeders from all over the world, all muddled together. I need to narrow this down. But how? On an impulse, I type in "Arizona Shih Tzu breeders" and hit Search.

Another list of links appears and I click on the first thing that isn't an advertisement. This brings me to the Arizona Shih Tzu Home Page and a photograph of a couple and a little boy – all three of them wearing red shirts – and five Shih Tzus, two of them with red bows in their topknots. The woman has striking, long, honey-blonde hair like the kind you see in TV adver- tisements, and the man sports a mustache and granny glasses. Their names are Jeri and Jackson. The little boy is Colin, their grandson. It is a really sweet photograph, good enough to be a Christmas card. I wonder how the photographer managed to get all five of the Shih Tzus to look at the camera at the same time. They're all beautiful little dogs. Except for his little Fu Manchu "mustache" the one at the center of the photograph looks just like Bao.

This is it. This is where I'm going to find him.

But wait a minute. Come on. This is just too simple, too perfect. Things don't happen this way in real life, I tell myself. You're supposed to be making a list. Stick to the plan. The American Kennel Club probably has lists of breeders. Try them.

This doesn't work. It's against AKC policy to identify – much less recommend –individual breeders. Instead, they offer contact information for volunteer groups called AKC Parent Clubs. There's one of these for each breed.

I click my way to the American Shih Tzu Club's website. It is well organized and informative, but it does not offer any information about breeders. Instead, there are half a dozen Breeder Referral Committee Members. Their headquarters are in San Francisco. I call, get a recorded message and leave a message of my own, explaining that I'm looking for a Shih Tzu breeder in Arizona. Nobody calls back.

Over the next few days I try again and again, always getting the same recorded message. So I go back to the website and tackle the list of Breeder Referral Committee Members, who are scattered all over the United States. Members of the public are warned that telephone calls will be returned collect.

Most of the Committee Members aren't home and don't have answering machines. I finally reach someone in California. She's very pleasant, very helpful, and not surprised that nobody is answering the telephone at Headquarters. "The woman who was doing that job for us hasn't been well for some time. You have to remember that we're all volunteers," she tells me. "And most of us are getting on in years."

I explain that I live in Arizona and want to buy a puppy. She replies that she's not sure how she can help me, because it's against American Shih Tzu Club policy to provide names of individual breeders. "If you're looking for that kind of information," she says, "you have to approach your state organization. And in your case that's the problem, because Arizona doesn't have a state organization. I don't know why. Maybe, nobody could be bothered. We're all volunteers, as I told you. Or it could be that Arizona breeders aren't able to meet AKC standards."

"But there are people here in Arizona selling AKC-registered Shih Tzus," I protest. "I just saw a web-site."

"Yes, but anyone can put up a website. And they can say all kinds of wonderful things about their kennels and their champion dogs, but it doesn't mean anything. You can build a website in a couple of hours, if you know what you're doing. Then, all you have to do is steal a few photographs of prize-winning dogs and puppies from legitimate breeders, and post them. Drag and drop, it's as easy as that. My five year old grandson can do it. And who's going to know the difference? I'm not trying to discourage you, dear. But you really do have to be careful, these days. A lot of those websites you're talking about are probably just fronts for puppy mills, or even for people who are selling stolen dogs."

Jeri, Jackson and Colin don't look like people who are fronting for a puppy mill, much less selling stolen dogs. But she has a point. Anyone can put anything on the internet.

She can't recommend any breeders in Arizona. "And I have to tell you, the fact there's no state organization is not a good sign. Personally, I can't recall ever having even met a breeder from Arizona. But that's going back a few years," she adds. "Besides, I don't even breed Shih Tzus, anymore. I retired a few years ago. So maybe I'm not the best person to ask. What I can do is to give you the names and telephone numbers of a few breeders I know in Nevada and California. But I should warn you, a lot of them may be retired, like I am."

I write down the names and telephone numbers, and thank her. But it feels wrong. You know that feeling when you're driving along an unfamiliar dark road and you come to a T-intersection and there are no signs? You take a left – or a right – and within minutes you know you're going the wrong way.

But I keep going, working my way through the list of breeders I've been given because I can't think of anything better. Some of the telephone numbers have been disconnected, or belong to other people. Others aren't home. Only one of them has an answering machine. (I leave a message, which is never returned) The last person on the list answers her telephone and says she's still breeding Shih Tzus. And yes, she has some lovely puppies for sale.

"But I'm going to be very honest with you," she continues. "I'm extremely busy, and I can't see the point in either of us wasting our time. The first thing you need to know is that all of my puppies are show quality. The prices start at $1750 and they are not negotiable."

I assure her that price isn't a problem. "And I'm not looking for a show dog, either."

It's the wrong thing to say.

"If you don't want to show the dog, then why are you contacting a reputable breeder like me and taking up my time? To have a perfect dog and not show it is a waste. It's a crime, that's what it is. Do you have the slightest idea of how much time and effort and expertise and expense goes into breeding a show quality Shih Tzu? I wouldn't even consider selling one of my wonderful puppies to a person like you, who wasn't going to show it. If all you want is a pet, why don't you just go to a pet store and buy a mutt? Or adopt one, from a shelter?" Her voice rises with exasperation. "My puppies aren't pets! My puppies are champions!"

Thoroughly disheartened, I pour myself a glass of wine and sit down on the couch. This isn't working. I look at a photograph of Bao. His beautiful, brown eyes gaze lovingly back at me. What am I doing wrong? How am I going to find you?

Perhaps I'm over-thinking. Perhaps I'm being too rational, following my mind rather than my heart. First, the universe gives you a nudge. Then, a poke. Then, a slap. It's time to get out of my own way, and let the universe do its job.

Back at Arizona Shih Tzu, Jeri, Jackson and Colin seem to be waiting for me. This time I explore the whole website, lingering over the "Nursery" page and the wonderful photos of wide-eyed puppies sprawled on pillows or posed in chocolate boxes or coffee cups. Shih Tzu puppies are adorable. Looking at them brings back happy memories, and I find myself smiling. None of these beautiful little creatures is Bao, of course. He hasn't been born yet.

One of the dogs on the "Mommies and Mommies To Be" page looks so much like Bao that she could be his sister. Her name is Carmella. Impulsively, I send off an email, asking if Carmella is due to have a litter in August. Jeri replies a few hours later. Carmella isn't expecting, and they don't plan to mate her before Thanksgiving. But there are some beautiful puppies available right now, and another litter due early in July. If I'm interested in a puppy, the first thing I need to do is complete one of their Arizona Shih Tzu questionnaires, which she's attached.

I'm not surprised, or even disappointed. If it isn't Carmella it will be one of the others. At least, I know where my puppy is going to be born. I save the questionnaire for later.

Meanwhile, my own dear Bao is gone. It hurts every time my gaze falls upon his water dish (which I still keep filled with fresh water) and every time I look up and he isn't there. Even when he does come back to me, he'll be another dog living a completely different life.

Christians believe in an immortal, individual, unchanging soul, but Buddhists believe in something more ephemeral which they call a "continuity of consciousness" created by the circumstances of each of our lives and continually transforming, like waves that rise, break and subside. It is this continuity of consciousness – rather than a single, individualistic ego – that reincarnates, moving from one life to the next the way a caterpillar moves from one blade of grass to another. The Dalai Lama explains it this way: "The successive existences as a series of rebirths are not like the pearls in a pearl necklace, held together by a string, the 'soul' which passes through all the pearls; rather they are like dice, piled one on top of the other. Each die is separate, but it supports the one above it, with which it is functionally connected."

The Dalai Lama would say I'm selfish for wanting Bao to come back as a dog, rather than enjoy a human rebirth. Being born into the animal realm is not considered as good a rebirth as being born human. This is because although animals can do good or bad things, only human beings consciously choose to be good or bad and it is this choice – or intention – that constitutes virtue and creates karma. "This is why," writes the Dalai Lama, "that although many types of being have evolved upon this planet since its formation, those who have brought about the most improvement are human beings, and those who have learned how to create the most fear, suffering and other problems – threatening even the destruction of the planet – are also humans. The best is being done by humans and the worst is being done by humans."

Dalai Lama or no Dalai Lama, I don't feel guilty about wanting Bao to come back to me. Besides, it's too late. He's already on his way.

Meanwhile, the days are slow and sorrowful. I can't concentrate. Everything in my condo reminds me of Bao. In the months after Rollyn died I'd found some respite from grief in long, long walks. But going outdoors in southern Arizona at this time of year is like walking into an oven. People who don't live here just can't imagine what it's like during the summer. It's not just a few days of hot weather. It is weeks on end of temperatures over a hundred and ten degrees. And there's no respite. The streets and sidewalks absorb the heat and radiate it back, so that it never really cools off, not even at night. That's why everyone goes away.

Bao and I used to go away, as well. One summer, we toured the National Parks. Another summer, we went to the Shakespeare Festival in Stratford, Canada. Last year, we went to Northern California. Bao loved car trips, and he was a wonderful traveling companion.

But heat or no heat, dogs have to do what dogs have to do. During the summer months we always walked early in the morning, just after the sun rose, and then again at twilight. But without Bao, I have no reason to go outdoors and so I'm spending long, silent days alone, sitting on the couch watching television and drinking too much wine.

Jeannie and Bob are going to their place in Rocky Point for a week. "Why don't you come, too? You haven't been down since before Bao got sick, have you? If you want, Bob and I can check your condo for you, just to make sure everything is okay. But you know what? I think you should come. You need to get out."

Like Jeannie, I own a beachfront condominium in Rocky Point (or Puerto Penasco) just over the border and an easy, four hour drive from Scottsdale. I bought it seven years ago. In fact, that's how I met Jeannie – I ended up buying her condo when she bought a larger one. And I have always loved the beach, and the sea. Bao and I often went to Rocky Point for a week or more at a time, and at one point (when I still lived in Tucson) I even considered moving there permanently.

I've never been to Rocky Point without Bao. My first thought is that it will just be another place full of memories, and I don't know if I can handle it. But it isn't all that far, and there's nothing to stop me coming back to Scottsdale if it's too painful. I bring Bao's leash and harness along with me, as well as a framed photograph that was taken just days before he got sick. And I talk to him during the drive and when we stop for gas in Ajo, as I always did.

But the first few hours after we arrived are really, really difficult. All the Mexican staff at the Sonoran Spa have known Bao for years, and many of them loved him almost as much as I did. So naturally, everyone wants to know where he is. Again and again, I explain (in halting Spanish) that he's gone, that he'd died two weeks ago, that his heart had stopped beating and the doctors couldn't make it start again. I'd memorized the Spanish words before I left Scottsdale, because I knew everybody would ask. I still can't talk about it without crying, and many of the women weep with me. They are so kind to me. They say, Lo siento – and they hug me.

The condo seems hollow and quiet. I fill Bao's water dish, as I always do. And I hang his leash and harness in their usual place on the door. His little wicker basket full of toys is there by the window, just as we'd left it. I can feel his presence, very strongly. It's almost as if he's glad to be here.

The balcony of my condo has a raised banquette running the length of it. I've got cushions for it, which I always bring inside when I'm not here, so they won't fade. I put them back as soon as I arrive and this was one of our rituals, unlocking the condo and opening the sliders and putting the cushions on the banquette. Bao made a game of it, eagerly leaping up on the cushions as I put them down so that he could lie in the sun and watch the comings and goings on the beach far below.

I begin to cry as I put the cushions in place, thinking of him. In my mind's eye, I imagine him leaping happily up onto his favorite cushion, settling himself and staring out at his beach, his ocean. And he's here, after all. I can feel him. I sit down next to where he would be if he was here physically, and gaze out at the sea. We used to love sitting here in the sun, watching the waves and the people on the beach.

Being here isn't as bad I'd thought it would be. It's high tide, and the gulls are swooping and diving, catching fish.

I pour myself a Scotch, and watch the sunset.

Bao is not with me all the time, but he's with me now. I expected that coming here without him would be unbearable, but I'm not without him. He's in my heart and he's also a presence, a psychic presence. He's somehow telling me it's okay, but without language.

The doggy steps are still in place pushed up against the side of the bed. The little dish that I kept filled with kibble (for midnight snacks) is still here and I'm tempted to fill it with kibble and put it on the bed, the way I always did. But I don't. Instead, I look at Bao's photograph, which I've propped on the night stand. I kiss his dear little face and turn out the light and close my eyes.

The ocean is just yards away and one of the things I like most about being here is being able to leave the sliding glass doors open so I can fall asleep to the sound of the sea. But tonight a group of women renting the condo directly below mine is celebrating something, playing loud music and shrieking with laughter. Even with the doors shut, I can still hear the racket. Some people go wild when they come to Mexico, behaving in ways they'd never behave at home. Jeannie says people don't have manners anymore, and maybe she's right. Or maybe we're just getting old. When I finally do fall asleep, it's almost morning.

The next day I'm tired, irritable and out of sorts. I don't feel like walking on the beach, or going for a swim or doing much of anything. When I sold my house in Tucson and moved to a condo in Scottsdale, a lot of my books ended up here in Mexico. My eyes fall upon a boxed set still wrapped in cellophane. Meditation for Beginners.

I meditated for the first time 25 years ago, while I still lived in Australia. I'd attended a seminar presented by Ian Gawler, who was diagnosed with terminal cancer and had turned to meditation when doctors had nothing more to offer. Eventually, his cancer disappeared. Gawler subsequently funded the Melbourne Cancer Support Group, wrote books and presented seminars like this one. We did a group meditation during which hundreds of us closed our eyes and meditated for about 20 minutes. I thought it was interesting, although I never quite got around to meditating on my own. However, when I saw these books in a sale some years later, I bought them.

Now, I tear off the cellophane and open the box, which contains a spiral-bound manual and two CDs. Settling myself comfortably on a cushion, I play the first CD, a guided meditation. There's gentle music. A soothing, quiet voice tells me to begin by making myself comfortable and closing my eyes and just listening, becoming aware of the sounds in my environment. Little waves hitting the sand, the cry of a sea bird, a dog on the beach, barking. Just listening. I do this for a while. Then the voice tells me to begin to pay attention to my breathing, to the feeling of my breath in my nostrils as I inhale and exhale. That's all, says the voice. Just your breath.

It isn't what I'd expected, but it is certainly easy enough to do. So I sit there feeling my breath fill my lungs, feeling it leave my lungs and move through my nostrils. I notice the space between breaths. I have never really paid attention to my breath, before. My mind wanders to other things. Concentrate on your breath, says the voice. If your attention begins to wander, bring it gently back to your breath. I do, but moments later I find myself wondering whether the horrible women renting the condo downstairs will be there again tonight. And whether or not I ought to complain to Management about the noise. Again, the quiet voice reminds me to bring my attention back to my breath. You'd think just paying attention to your breath would be easy, but it isn't. The thoughts just keep coming. Years ago, a Buddhist friend told me that I had a chattering, monkey mind. Now I understand what he meant.

The track comes to an end. I open my eyes, and unfold my legs. Half an hour has passed, and that surprises me. I would have thought I'd be bored, sitting for half an hour with my eyes closed and trying to think of nothing. If anything, I feel serene, and that surprises me, too. Any minute it'll start hurting again, I think. But it doesn't. Instead, I have the completely crazy feeling that Bao approves, that meditation is something he wants me to do. I gaze across the room at his photograph, and he gazes back at me.

Bao is here. Bao is all around me. It's almost like the feeling that enveloped me during the drive home from Colorado, the absolute, unquestioning certainty that Bao's psychic presence was in the car with me and that

Bao himself was on his way back to me. I continue to sit very quietly, because I want the feeling to last.

The manual is lying next to me and I open it and begin to read. Meditation, I learn, is about learning how to be wholly in the present moment. Mostly, we spend our lives remembering, or anticipating. Yet in reality, we only live one second at a time. This moment – right now – is all we have. The past is gone. The future hasn't arrived. There is only this moment, this breath.

I sit reading for an hour or so and then I go for a swim in the pool. There's hardly anyone around. I' ve got the pool to myself and while I'm swimming I think about mindfulness. I feel the warm water slapping against my arms and legs, and the hot, afternoon sun on my back. I swim mindfully, back and forth across the otherwise deserted pool. I can almost believe that if I look up, I'll see Bao curled up on one of the deck chairs, watching me. Of course, I can't. Yet, he's here with me. I can feel him, as surely as I feel the water, and the sun.

Though most of my life, I've lived in coastal cities – Miami, Los Angeles, San Francisco, Kailua, Sydney. I've always loved the beach, and the rhythms of waves and tide. There's something about the sound of the waves hitting the sand, something about the salt air. Back upstairs on my balcony, I sit and watch the changing patterns of the sea. Here, there are only natural sounds. The waves. The birds. The breeze clicking softly through the palm fronds. They say that the sea, the mountains and waterfalls all emit a special, healing energy.

I'm still sad. I still miss Bao. But something has shifted. Perhaps it's the absence of traffic noise and electronic devices, or the gentle, pulsing rhythm of the falling tide. Jeannie was right. I did need a change. This is a good place to be. I decide to try to meditate every day, even if it's only for a few minutes.

> *Bao's psychic presence is very strong, very comforting, so much so that I find myself thinking that perhaps this is all I need, maybe he doesn't have to take on a physical body in order to be with me. But does that mean he doesn't want me to look for him? No, I think it means that he's comforting me and making certain that I don't look for him until he's ready. If he's already growing inside his mother, they won't even be sure she's pregnant, yet. I'm so lonely ...*

The following evening my friend Judy invites me to her place for dinner. I originally met Judy when we were both living in Tucson and doing volunteer work at the Tucson Museum of Art, but I only really got to know her after she moved to Rocky Point. Like all my friends, Judy was devastated to hear about Bao's death. He loved coming to see her, and she even assembled a little basket of toys for him to play with when we visited. It's still there, when I walk in. And she's put water in his water dish, just like always.

Judy can feel Bao's presence, too. She believes in reincarnation and often communicates with her own beloved, dead husband. It is enormously comforting to be able to talk openly about my feelings with someone who is accustomed to experiencing these kind of spiritual phenomena and accepts them as part of human life. We talk about reincarnation over glasses of red wine, and wonder about our own past lives. Judy has no doubt whatsoever that Bao is coming back. "You've been together before," she said. "He was an old soul. And he loved you so much."

I feel comfortable about sharing my concerns with Judy. "I want him to come back to me. I want it so much. But I love him. I want what's best for him, too. And you know, Buddhists believe that all existence is suffering. And that animals can't perform spiritual practices and can't attain Enlightenment. So I shouldn't want him to come back as a dog, should I? Not if I really love him. But I **do** love him!"

"Of course you love him. And it can't just be about what you want," Judy said thoughtfully. "It's not only your karma. It's Bao's karma, too. And I think he wants to come back to you. He couldn't do that, if he was born human. He had a wonderful life with you. He had a better life than most people have, when you stop to think about it. And he loved you so much. Besides, just hours after his death, you said you knew he was coming back. So that makes it his choice, doesn't it?"

Later that night, lying in bed and listening to the murmur of the sea, I think about what Judy said. And I think about the terrible hour after Bao's death, sitting there in the quiet, darkened clinic, holding him in my arms, telling him again and again how much I loved him. In the twenty-first century, you're dead when the squiggly green line on the screen goes flat. The machines are switched off. All that's left is a corpse, a lifeless body awaiting burial or cremation. We get up and leave.

But according to Buddhist teaching, it's not over yet. The karmic body may have ceased to function, but the continuity of consciousness – the mind – continues for hours and even days after death.

Sogyal Rinpoche explains: "The outstanding feature of the bardo of becoming is that the mind takes on the predominant role ... and because the memory of our past karmic body is still fresh in our mind, we take on a "mental body". This mental body possesses all of its senses, but it is also light, lucid and clairvoyant. It is also extremely restless, unable to stay still. And it can go wherever it wants to go, just by thinking.

Certainly, as I sat there holding him I could feel Bao's mental body. He could hear me. He could see me. He knew I was holding him. He was no longer in his body, but he was there. He knew how much I loved him.

I love you, I kept saying. I love you so much. I love you to the moon and back. And I will always love you, always and forever. After an hour, I felt that it was time to go. But I didn't leave Bao behind. He came back to the motel with me, because he wanted to and because he could.

People who have near death experiences confirm that life does not end when the machines flatline. Deepak Chopra writes about Mellen-Thomas Benedict, who died of a brain tumor in 1982 and was clinically dead for 90 minutes. Benedict vividly remembers leaving his body, going into the light, and journeying through multiple layers of cosmic awareness. "It came to him that he could see to infinity. He was in the void, or pre-creation as he calls it, and his consciousness was limitless. He was in contact with the absolute, which wasn't a religious experience but one of unbounded awareness. He perceived all of creation generating itself without beginning or end. Instead of one Big Bang, a singular event that created the universe, Benedict perceived millions of big bangs constantly generating new universes. Since he was beyond time, this was happening simultaneously in all dimensions." When Benedict woke up, the tumor was gone.

13 million Americans have had near death experiences. Some have written books about it. Again, the evidence is anecdotal. But it's pretty clear that something extraordinary happened to all of these people, and it is becoming obvious that the boundary between life and death is too complex to be measured by machines.

The next morning, I try to meditate again but I can't concentrate. So I decide to tackle the questionnaire Jeri sent me. It is quite long, and goes into much more detail than I expected. How much do I know about the Shih Tzu breed? Have I ever owned a Shih Tzu? How many hours per day do I expect to be able to devote to my Shih

Tzu puppy? What will he eat? Where will he sleep? Are there any other pets in the house? Any children? If so, how old are they? How old am I? How big is my back yard? Am I able to supply veterinary references?

It takes me over an hour to finish it, but I don't mind. I actually feel as if I'm finally doing something positive. The length and detail of the questionnaire reassures me. Clearly, a lot of thought and work has gone into it. Jeri and Jackson care about their puppies. That's good.

> *Thinking about Bao. All of my memories are good memories, and I cannot come to terms with this; I still feel his presence, against all rationality. It is a psychic presence, not a physical presence. When I let it, it comforts me. Where is he? In his mother's womb? Or still in the bardo of becoming? Lots of people believe that dogs reincarnate. Some people think the soul enters the body just before birth. Buddhists think it happens at conception. So do Catholics. Who knows what's true? But I have to believe that somehow, we'll find one another again.*

Jeannie and Bob have arrived, and we arrange to meet and walk the beach tomorrow morning when the tide is out. Puerto Penasco is on the Sea of Cortez, and the tides can be quite spectacular, especially when the moon is full and the water recedes so far that both of the volcanic, offshore reefs are exposed. Vast expanses of flat, hard sand appear. Dogs love it. They can run for miles, chasing a ball, barking at the sea birds and exploring the tidal pools. Other than the shrimp boats there isn't much industry in this part of Mexico, and the beach is wonderfully clean and – at low tide – covered with shells. From my balcony, I frequently see dolphins and sometimes, whales.

My condo is on the seventh floor and with binoculars, I can see for nearly a mile up and down the beach. Bao and I used to sit up here and watch Jeannie and her dogs – Cleopatra, Angelique and Tangerine – make their way down the beach towards us. The girls, I call them. Bao would lie with his nose between the railings, as if he could actually see them. Often, he knew they were coming even before I spotted them and I always wondered how he did that, because they say dogs don't have particularly good eyesight. Maybe he could smell them. Or maybe it was some kind of canine ESP.

I watch for them and when they are about a quarter of a mile away I go down to meet them, just as I always did. It seems strange, walking across the sand towards Jeannie and the girls without Bao scampering gleefully ahead of me. I had wondered how it would feel, seeing Jeannie's dogs alive and healthy, and knowing Bao was gone. I don't wish one of her dogs had died instead of mine, it isn't like that. On the other hand, I'm not completely sure I want to see them just yet. But Jeannie insists. She wants to see me. And it will do me good to get out and walk the beach.

It's already hot, but it's a beautiful morning. Cleopatra, Angelique and Tangerine frolic and chase their ball into the gently lapping waves. Watching them, I find myself smiling. Instead of making me feel sad, seeing "the girls" on the beach brings back happy memories of all the good times we shared with them. Bao enjoyed his life, right up to the very last day.

I tell Jeannie about Arizona Shih Tzu. I tell her about Carmella, and about sending an email asking if Carmella was going to have puppies. Jeannie wants to know if I have a "feeling" about any of the other Arizona Shih Tzu dogs, and I have to admit I don't. But I do know Bao is in a womb and on his way to being reborn. I'm sure about that. And I'm also sure I'll find him at Arizona Shih Tzu.

Jeannie is unconvinced, but hopeful. "At least, it's a start. It's better than sitting there by yourself and crying all day. And I hope you're right, I really do. You know that my whole background is in science. You know I don't believe in anything I can't see. But I could be wrong. And if it makes you feel better, I'm all for it."

Yes, I want to say, but even scientists recognize other modes of knowledge. What about quarks and gluons? Physicists infer them from traces left in bubble chambers, but nobody has ever actually seen one. And what about Albert Einstein's thought experiments? You can't see a thought experiment, either.

But Jeannie doesn't want to argue. "You don't have to persuade me, Gail. If you believe Bao is going to reincarnate, that's fine. And like I said, I hope you're right. You don't need to worry about what I believe. If it's going to happen, it'll happen whether I believe in it or not."

So we continue our walk along the beach, taking turns tossing the ball for the dogs and talking of other things.

When we say goodbye, she gives me a hug. "I've been worried about you. Weren't you working on a new book? I mean, before Bao got sick?" I nod. "Maybe you should try to get back into it. Look, I know how hard this is for you. Even after all these years, I still remember what it was like when I lost Saber. You'll never forget Bao, just the way I'll never forget Saber. And you shouldn't forget him. But you can't just stop living, either." She stops walking, and looks at me. "I just want to hear you laugh. I just want you to be happy again."

HOW TO HELP YOUR DOG REINCARNATE: WEEK FIVE

You've been doing this for weeks. Is it really going to work? And how long will it take? Shouldn't something have happened by now?

Friends may be telling you to stop brooding about your dog. He's gone, they say. No matter what you do, you can't bring him back. Thinking about him all the time isn't healthy. Read a book. Go see a movie. Have lunch with a friend.

They mean well. Perhaps you should listen to them. You still believe in reincarnation, but believing isn't knowing. Lots of people believe in reincarnation, but lots of other people don't. Who is right? How can anyone know for sure? You're doing your best, but nothing seems to be happening. Maybe nothing is ever going to happen. Maybe you should just stop.

You were confident at first. But it's been five weeks, and you're beginning to wonder. You're beginning to doubt.

There's nothing wrong with doubt, or doubting. You are a rational being. Doubt is part of the rational process. But you're doing now has nothing to do with rationality. It's based upon belief, and a belief cannot be right or wrong because a belief – by definition – is not rational.

We insist upon our rationality, our reasonableness. Yet we live according to our beliefs. Our laws are based upon morality, a set of beliefs that cannot be empirically validated. Asked to describe the United States, most Americans would mention things like liberty, equality, and democracy. These are not quantifiable. Nonetheless, we live by them and are willing to die for them. Rationality has its place, but it also has its limits.

So allow yourself to doubt, but don't let doubt transfix and immobilize you. You can entertain doubts, yet also continue to believe.

The Buddha tells a story about a man who is shot by a poisoned arrow. People rush to help him, but when someone tries to pull the arrow out, the man pushes him away. Wait! he cries. Before you pull it out I need to know where it came from. Who made it? What kind of poison did he use? And on and on, question after question, until finally, the arrow has remained in his body long enough to allow the poison to kill him. Doubt can be like that poisoned arrow.

But my dog is dead! How can I change that?

You can't. The past is history. There are no possibilities in the past, and that's the point. Reincarnation isn't about the past. Reincarnation is about the future, and the future is endless possibility. So long as nothing has happened, anything can happen.

Tomorrow, your dog may reincarnate and come back to you. This is what you need to think about. This is where you need to focus your attention. *My dog is going to come back to me. I'm going to find him, and I'm going to bring him home. We're going to be together, again.* You need to be saying this to yourself, over and over again.

In a sense, nothing can exist unless we think it into existence. Remember the paradox of the tree in the middle of the forest? One day, the tree falls. But nobody sees it fall. So did it fall? Or is it still standing? The answer is, both. If nobody has seen it, both possibilities continue to exist. What we perceive depends upon what we decide to perceive, upon attention and intention. Each of us creates our own reality, moment by moment.

"If you accept that your personal body is not separate from the universe," write Deepak Chopra and David Simon, "then by consciously changing the energy and informational content of your own body, you can influence the energy and information of your extended body – your environment, your world. This influence is activated by two qualities inherent in consciousness: Attention and intention. Attention enlivens, while intention transforms. If you want something to grow stronger in your life, direct more of your attention to it. If you want something to diminish in your life, withdraw your attention from it."

If your dog's karma is strong, won't he find his way back to you no matter what you do? Perhaps. But karma is not fate. It changes, as a result of action. Everything you think and do affects karma, and that includes paying attention. Not paying attention affects karma, as well.

So pay attention. You don't need to be thinking about your dog's reincarnation every minute of the day, but you do need to think about it. Do your job, care for your family, continue to live your life. But every so often during the day, stop and think about your dog. Think about how much you love him, and how much you want him to come back to you. For a few moments, pay attention.

If you want something to happen, you must name it. You must imagine it. You must envision it. The universe is infinite. Your dog is out there, somewhere. Believe, and pay attention. You will find him.

CHAPTER 6

Being in Rocky Point without Bao isn't any worse than being in Scottsdale without him. I still miss him terribly. But I continue to feel his presence, even though it is now nearly three weeks since I held him in my arms. The bond between us still exists, we are still connected. I think of it as a sort of spiritual lifeline stretched invisibly between us, linking our consciousnesses.

> *This morning, when I woke up, I was almost in what I would call a state of grace — calm, confident, free of pain. Not only will Bao come back to me, he is not really gone. He is simply in a different dimension. This has happened for a reason. There is something I must learn, something I could have learned in no other way, and when I have learned it, Bao will come back to me and be with me for the rest of my life. He was such a dear little dog. I loved him, I love him so much.*

Summers are often humid in Rocky Point, but even so, it's much more pleasant here by the sea than it is in Scottsdale at this time of year. At least you can go outdoors and it cools off at night. There's almost always a breeze off the ocean, as well.

I never tire of looking at the sea, which continually changes. One day, the water will be calm and still and I can see whole schools of fish swimming in the depths. The next morning I wake up to pounding surf and whitecaps. I like to sit outside with my coffee, watching the sun rise. Bao – his presence – is always here beside me on his favorite cushion. For some reason, mornings are our best time.

I don't want to give the impression that I think about Bao every minute of the day, because I don't. I read, and I watch television and I go back to translating some Chinese texts that interest me. I drive into town with Judy to buy buns at a Mexican bakery she's discovered, and we make a day of it, treating ourselves to lunch at Flavio's and then stocking up on shrimp and halibut from the stalls along the Malecon.

I have to consciously "pay attention" in order to become aware of Bao's psychic presence. In the first days after his death this happened spontaneously but now, I have to concentrate him into being. It's as if we are divided by an invisible vastness and must take turns sending pulses of energy into the void, always pausing to make sure the other one is still there and still listening. Attention is how we bridge the gap.

More and more, I feel attention and intention are actively creating a world in which Bao and I will be able to be together again. I don't mean this in a magical sense, but in the sense that each of us creates the world we inhabit, through paying attention to some things and ignoring others. Attention focusses energy. Thoughts and feelings reinforce one another. "When we hold a thought in our mind without being distracted," writes Madisyn Taylor, "we have achieved pure thought. When we have a positive emotional response to that thought, we enable it to dance and move and breathe itself into existence."

That is what is happening. My thoughts are dancing and moving and breathing themselves into existence.

And why not? We are all pure energy, we are all made of the same stuff. That's why I can still feel Bao's presence. His energy is reaching out to mine. We are vibrating on the same frequency.

The healthy human body vibrates at a frequency of 68 to 72 MHz. (Animals vibrate at a slightly lower frequency) While you're sitting here reading this, you are emitting a steady stream of vibrations, determined by your thoughts and feelings. So do other people. We vibrate in a sea of vibration.

We talk about "good vibes" and "bad vibes" and this is accurate, because the vibrations from other people can and do affect us. Positive thoughts and actions vibrate at higher frequencies, and attract higher frequencies. Negative thoughts vibrate at lower frequencies and can disrupt our own vibrations, throwing us into disharmony and literally causing dis-ease.

Ancient Chinese and Ayurvedic Indian medical practitioners recognized this, and learned how to use sound to rebalance and reharmonize, by associating specific notes with the corresponding subtle energy systems of the human body. Modern medical practitioners are rediscovering these techniques and using psychoacoustics (the study of the effects of sound upon the human consciousness) to promote healing.

You and I experience a narrow band of all this vibration as sound but mostly, we're not consciously aware of it. When we do manage to "tune in" it's often because we "have a premonition" that something is going to happen. (Usually, it's something bad. I wonder why. Maybe it's because we tend to dismiss our "good" premonitions as mere, wishful thinking.)

Animal communicators and psychics seem to possess a greater sensitivity that enables them to "tune in" to a range of vibrational frequencies, allowing them to do their special and specialized work. Are these people gifted, in the sense that great musicians and artists are said to be gifted? Or do we all possess a latent sensitivity for this sort of communication, only waiting to be developed?

I spend hours wondering about these things as I sit gazing at the sea. This is something new for me. I've never been one to sit around contemplating the invisible forces and inexplicable energies that shape the universe.

My father wouldn't tolerate such things. Why are you just sitting there? he'd ask. Haven't you got something to do? All my life, there has always been something to do. Win a scholarship. Get a job. Find a husband. Buy a house. Raise your kids. Sell your books.

And for what? Where did it all get me, in the end? Tears fill my eyes. I'd give it all – every bit of it – just to have Bao back again. And suddenly, here he is at my side. I don't have to look. I can feel him.

I do not pretend to understand. I simply know what I know and for now, that's enough.

As the sun sets I sit sipping wine, watching a breeze chase ripples across the surface of the sea. I stay in Rocky Point for a few more days, and then return to Scottsdale and my empty condo.

I am becoming inured to the great emptiness in my life, although I still feel him near me, trying to comfort me. There are even moments of – not pleasure – but painlessness. The most awful thing is that I can't do anything for him, I can't show him how much I love him. Yet I keep seeing him, feeling him in a womb, in a dark, warm, cozy, safe place, growing and waiting to be born.

Back in Scottsdale, I continue to meditate. I am discovering that one of the things that happens while I'm meditating is that I become aware of my thoughts, of the fact that although my body is sitting quietly, my mind is bouncing from one thought to the next. My thoughts are hectic and disorderly, jumping from one topic to the next. One minute I'm concentrating on by breathing. The next minute I'm thinking about the sale at Macy's and wondering if I should buy a crockpot. I drag my thoughts back to my breath but a moment later, I'm wondering how those non-surgical face lifts work. Is this really meditating? The instruction manual says it is.

It occurs to me that if I'm aware of my thoughts I can't **be** my thoughts. This thing I call "I" must be something else. I studied Descartes in Philosophy 101. I think, therefore I am. But who am I, if I'm not my thoughts?

Most days I use the guided meditations, but I've also begun to experiment with meditating on my own, just closing my eyes and trying to concentrate on each breath. In some ways, this is easier. I find myself getting into a sort of rhythm, the rising and falling of my breath like the rocking of a cradle. I like the way I feel afterwards so I keep on doing it.

These final days of June are long, and empty. The sun rises early and by mid-morning I can see heat mirages shimmering above the asphalt. Somebody's visiting grandchildren try to fry an egg on the pavement next to the swimming pool, but they don't swim. The water is too warm. By noon, our beautifully landscaped grounds are deserted. Everyone is indoors, or at the mall.

I haven't heard back from Arizona Shih Tzu since I sent them my completed questionnaire. It's been a week. Shouldn't someone have contacted me, if only to say they'd received the questionnaire? What if they've rejected me? What if they think I'm too old for a puppy?

This is possible. I can appreciate how Jeri and Jackson might feel this way. But shouldn't they at least give me a chance to present my side of the story? I'm healthy and fit. I took good care of Bao. Besides, it's not as if the puppy will be a puppy forever. Puppies grow up. I spend most of the day engaged in an imaginary argument with Jeri, trying to persuade her to sell me a puppy, and then I telephone.

Jeri answers, explaining that she's been visiting family in Michigan and is still working through the pile of email that accumulated in her absence. But she's glad I called because she was meaning to contact me, in any case. There's a new litter of puppies about to be born. Might I be I interested in putting a deposit on one of them?

"It's too soon," I tell her.

There's a silence.

"My puppy won't be born until after July 27th."

Another silence

I suddenly realize how strange this must sound. Obviously, I'm going to have to explain. But where do I begin? I've never met Jeri and Jackson, and they've never met me and I don't want to come across as some kind of nut. Carefully choosing my words, I tell Jeri the whole story, beginning with Bao's death. I tell her about his ongoing, psychic presence and my conviction that he will be reborn, my certainty that he is already in his mother's womb. I even tell her about the breeder of champion

Shih Tzus, who refused to sell me a puppy if I wasn't going to show it. Jeri laughs, which breaks the ice a bit. "The thing is," I conclude, "conception couldn't take place before Bao died. At least, I don't think it could. So that's why I think he'll be born in August."

When I finish, there is another long silence. I hear Jeri take a deep breath and realize she is also choosing her words. She begins by saying she's always been a person who respects other people's beliefs. "The problem is, I don't think we're going to have another litter so soon after the puppies that are coming next week. In fact, we might not have another litter until September. You can put two dogs together, but it doesn't always take. And even if the mating is successful, all kinds of things can happen during a pregnancy. You just never know until the last few weeks and sometimes, not even then. I never tell people we're going to have a litter until I'm absolutely sure, because I don't want to disappoint them. Jackson and I are going away again, so we'll be gone during the first two weeks of July. But I've got your telephone number and I'll get back to you as soon as I'm sure we've got some puppies on the way."

At least they haven't rejected me. They don't think I'm too old to take on a puppy. That's a relief. I agree to send Jeri a deposit, because I want first choice of the next litter, even if I have to wait until September. But I don't think I will. If Bao is already in his mother's womb, he'll be born in August. And he'll be a boy. I hadn't known that, but now – somehow – I do.

After I hang up, I go into my study and sit down at my desk, but I can't bring myself to write the check. My husband used to tease me about the way I make decisions. "Most people worry. They weigh up the pros and cons and agonize over whether they're doing the right thing, and then finally, they decide. But you're just the opposite. First, you decide, and then afterwards, you worry."

I sit there staring into space. How can I even think of bringing another dog into Bao's house?

But won't be another dog. It'll be Bao.

Do I **really** believe this?

When the Dalai Lama dies, everyone takes it for granted that he'll reincarnate. The monks make inquiries throughout Tibet, looking for births that have been preceded by special signs, or perhaps special dreams. After the death of the last Dalai Lama a rainbow pointed east, suggesting the rebirth would also occur in the east. Divinations were performed. Search parties were sent out to find and test potential candidates. Nobody suggested that the reincarnation of the Dalai Lama was impossible. But I'm not the Dalai Lama. I'm not a Buddhist monk. I'm not even a very good Buddhist.

Will he really come back to me? This morning he seems totally irreplaceable (which he is) and even the thought of another dog seems a betrayal. But if his soul has been reborn? We are meant to be together, I feel that so strongly.

But another dog, a puppy – will it be fair to the puppy? Will I ever be able to love it the way I loved, the way I still love Bao? Yes, if it is Bao. But how will I know? I want him to come back to me, I believe he will come back to me (in fact, that he's already on his way back to me even as I write these words) I believe such things can be – but I am also shaped by my time and place and what we call rationality. More than anything else, I don't want to betray him with another dog. But if he's on his way back to me and I don't look for him and find him and bring him home – isn't that a betrayal as well?

I leave my study, and wander back into the living room and sit down on the couch. The sun blazes down. Nothing stirs on my patio. The sky is cloudlessly blue, as if it was painted. The vivid, tropical greenery looks painted, too. The whole scene could be one of those backdrops they used to paint for movies. How do we know what is real, and what isn't? I begin to feel Bao's presence. He's simply here, the way he was always at my feet or under my chair when he was alive. But am I really feeling this? Or is it just my imagination?

Maybe I shouldn't send a check, make a deposit on a puppy. Maybe he isn't coming back to me. How can I possibly get another dog? How could any dog live up to Bao? And a puppy – housebreaking it, training it. Am I up for that? Maybe I should just live with my wonderful

memories and be grateful to have them. Yet there's some-
thing else, this strong feeling that I should keep moving
forward, towards this puppy that hasn't been born yet. If
we are truly meant to be together again, we will be.

Late that afternoon, I do write the check. But it takes
me a few more days to address the envelope, and another
day to mail it.

The next morning, our concierge telephones to tell
me I've got a package. Four weeks ago, Bao would have
leapt up and followed me to the door, eagerly wagging
his tail. Now, I'm going downstairs alone to get his ashes.
I'm almost afraid to open the box, afraid of what I'll
find. Whoever has done this has been gentle, and caring.
Bao's ashes are in an attractive, coffin-shaped little box
with a spray of artificial flowers affixed to the top. I put it
on the table beneath his portrait, reminding myself Bao's
ashes are not Bao. They are the remains of his body, and
there is a difference between body and soul. I am not
nearly as upset as I thought I would be. I'm glad his ashes
are with me. When I die, our ashes will be mingled. For
now, I'm glad he's home.

It has been over four weeks and by now, I should be
accustomed to him not being here anymore. But I'm not,
not at all. I'm still heartbroken. You don't just get over
the death of a beloved dog. When Frederick the Great
lost his dog Biche, he wrote: "I have lost Biche ... I was
ashamed that a dog could so deeply affect my soul; but
the sedentary life that I lead and faithfulness of this poor

creature had so strongly attached me to her, her suffering so moved me, that, I confuss, I am sad and afflicted. Does one have to be hard? Must one be insensitive? I believe that anyone capable of indifference to a faithful animal is unable to be grateful towards an equal, and that, if one must choose, it is best to be too sensitive than too hard."

I'm not eating much and I'm not sleeping well, although I'm going through the motions, getting my hair done and paying the bills. Jeannie continues to call every day. She's at her wit's end, wanting to help but not knowing how. What can she say? What can she do? What can anyone do? Bao is gone.

I tell her about my recent conversation with Jeri.

"Don't you want to go and look at the puppies? I can come along with you, and we could do lunch afterwards."

"It's too soon. Bao won't be born until the beginning of August."

"But the woman said there weren't going to be any more puppies born until September, didn't she?"

"Not exactly. She said she doesn't like to tell people there'll be puppies until she's sure."

"So when will she be sure?"

"Not for a while, I guess. She's going away again and she won't be back until mid-July."

Jeannie heaves a sigh. "So let's say you're right, and he'll be born in August. You know you'll have to wait eight weeks until he's old enough to leave his mother, don't you?" I know that, yes. "So that'll be ... what? Late September? That's months from now!"

"I can't help it."

"And I can't stand the thought of you sitting there alone in that condo for the next three months. You love to travel. You've always loved to travel, ever since I've known you. You know what I think? I think you should take a trip."

"I just got back from Rocky Point."

"No, I mean a real trip. You once said you'd always wanted to go to India, but you couldn't, because you didn't want to leave Bao. So why don't you do that? Why don't you go to India?"

India?

"Bao was a wonderful little dog, and nobody loved him more than I did. But he's gone, Gail. You've got to start living your life again." I don't know what to say. "It doesn't have to be India," Jeannie continues. "It can be anyplace you've always wanted to go. What about Tibet? Have you ever been to Tibet?"

I've never been to Tibet. There are so many places I've never visited, so many sights I've never seen. Venice. Scandinavia. The Amazon. Antarctica. But it doesn't matter. I don't care, anymore. I don't care about anything.

"At least say you'll think about it," Jeannie says.

"Okay. I'll think about it."

I do love to travel. But the most important thing in my life right now is Bao's psychic presence, and – although I can't explain why – I think he can only be with me in places we've already been. If I was to go to off to India or Tibet, he might not be able to follow. Our spiritual connection might weaken, or even disappear. And then what? Would he still be able to come back to me?

This is irrational, and I know it. Logically speaking, a psychic presence ought to be able to go anywhere. Otherwise, what would be the point of being psychic? But that's how I feel, and I can't help it. Besides, there's nothing logical about any of this. I'm in a place where intuition – rather than reason – rules.

This morning, I am more at peace than I have been since Bao left me. Bao has a karmic destiny, too. And although he isn't "here" he isn't "gone", either. Instead of intellectually picking this new feeling of peace to bits, I should try to simply rest in it. Truly, I am better today. I don't love Bao any less and I don't miss him any less, but the pain has eased. I almost feel as if there was some turning-point, some kind of crisis (perhaps his mother almost miscarried) but he's safely past it now, safe and growing in his mother's womb, getting ready to be reborn. Sadness comes in bursts, like the blow of an invisible fist. Meditating helps. So does anticipation of Bao coming back to me, the puppy growing in the womb, who will be born in August.

Days drag past. The Summer Solstice comes and goes and June becomes July. I'm restless, and bored. Nothing interests me for very long, and I'm sick of Lifetime movies. It'll be weeks before I hear anything more from Jeri. I don't know if Bao is going to be reborn early in

August – as I am so certain he will be – or not. Even if he is, there's still all of July to get through. I decide to go back to Mexico.

At least it's cooler in Rocky Point, although by now daytime temperatures are in the high eighties and the humidity is awesome, softening my skin and frizzing my hair. But even on the hottest days there's always a breeze off the ocean. Early in the morning and again at sunset, it's cool enough to walk the beach.

Every morning, I check my computer for a message from Arizona Shih Tzu, just in case. But there's nothing. I read, and meditate, and take long walks on the beach. For some reason, the psychic link between me and Bao seems stronger here. Or perhaps he's just getting closer to being reborn.

I know he'll be a different dog in a different body. After all, if we simply repeated our lives again and again, what would be the point of reincarnation? So he will and won't be Bao. He won't be called Bao, either. He'll have his own name, although I have no idea at all of what that might be. I wonder what he'll look like, this time around. Most often, Shih Tzus are black and white, or tan and white. Bao was blonde, the color of champagne. People always noticed him and said how beautiful he was. He knew exactly what they were staying, and lapped it up. He loved being beautiful. It doesn't matter to me, what he'll look like. But some-how, I think it matters to him. I think he wants to be beautiful again.

I miss Bao, sadly rather than painfully, and am comforted by reading texts that buttress my belief that he is growing towards rebirth, coming back to me. Certainly he is "holding" me, invisibly and from afar – but I feel him and this feeling is what has made the unbearable pain bearable. Bao (as he was) is gone. Bao and I (as we were) are ended. But nothing is ever gone, especially love. Nothing is ended. What's important is immortal, and is always present in one way or another. Bao (everything that made him Bao) is coming back to me. This is not what they call bargaining. This is what is. In a thousand different ways, Bao is reassuring me.

When I return from Mexico, there's another package from Colorado waiting for me. The staff at the veterinary hospital found the stuffed toy that comforted Bao on that last night, and they thought I'd want it. I'm not so sure. I'm afraid the sight of it will tear my heart out. But when I open the package and hug it close to me, I feel peaceful, and very close to him.

In less than two weeks, Jeri will be back. And of course, I remind myself, Bao may not be born in August. It may have taken him longer to find the right parents, and the right place. I might have to wait until September, or even October. But I don't think so. I have such a strong feeling that he went straight to his mother's womb, that he is on his way back to me.

Incredibly, five weeks have passed. The searing anguish of loss has gradually become a deep, aching sadness. I no longer burst into tears every time I think of

Bao, although I still can't talk about him without choking up. My ability to concentrate is improving. Maybe, I think, I should go back to the novel I'd been writing when Bao got sick. I pull it up on the computer, but it's too soon.

I am still very aware of Bao's psychic presence, especially in the morning when I first wake up.

Last night I dreamed about a clearing in the woods and a path that led to a vast body of water, with a couch built into the wall that overlooked it. And there was a deer, lying down at the head of the path. I was afraid it was hurt, or dead. But when I reached out and touched it I realized it was alive, it was all right. And – in a different dream – a long, misjudged walk. I'd tried to walk to a destination but had misjudged the distance and by the time I realized this it was too late to do anything, so I had to just keep going. I knew I wouldn't get back home until terribly late, but I told myself that wasn't a catastrophe, because I had nothing I had to do until tomorrow night.

What do these dreams mean? I once wrote a children's book about a baby gazelle. The point of the book was that sometimes you've just got to wait, and believe. So that makes sense, sort of. But the other dream, the one about the long walk and getting lost. What might that mean?

Some friends from Tucson drive up to Scottsdale for the day and we meet for lunch. They know that Bao is gone, of course. And they know how much I loved him. They're sorry. They know how hard it must be for me. If there is anything either of them can do to help, I have only to ask. We go on to talk of other things, mutual friends and Chinese art and whether the economy is finally picking up. After they've left, I am proud of myself. Several weeks ago, I'd have been dreadful company, incapable of social interaction and impatient with small talk.

But a few hours later, I crash. Everything is meaningless. The best and happiest part of my life is over. From here on, nothing will ever be as good as it had been. Bao is gone, and he is never coming back. All that's left are his ashes.

I cry until there are no more tears. Then I try to meditate. I close my eyes, and concentrate on my breath and suddenly, Bao is here on the couch beside me. I can feel his warm little body, curled against my hip. We'll get through this, I whisper to him. We will get through this.

So you see, it wasn't all miracle and epiphany. There were plenty of bleak, dark times as well. I was not always strong and confident. I questioned. I doubted. Sometimes, I wondered if I was going mad. Writing it down like this sometimes makes it sound as if it was all quite simple and straightforward, but it wasn't. There were many times when the only thing I felt was utter despair.

Perhaps if I was one of those Tibetan monks whose dogs always reincarnate it would be easier, just a matter of waiting quietly and serenely for Bao to return to me. But I am not a Tibetan monk. Again and again, I am overwhelmed by negative emotions and a sense of hopelessness.

I've begun to be apprehensive, as well. Bao is an embryo growing in his mother's womb, and there are so many things that can go wrong. What if his mother gets hurt, or sick?

Meditation helps, because I'm learning how to control my thoughts. I don't have to be afraid. I can make a conscious choice to focus my attention upon my certainty that Bao is coming back to me rather than upon all my doubts and fears. I can choose to send good, positive energy into the universe, and when I do, Bao feels it and moves towards it, and towards me. Of course, it's not as easy as that. It's not easy at all. But at least, it's my choice. It is something I can do.

HOW TO HELP YOUR DOG REINCARNATE: WEEK SIX

Feeling awful and doubting everything doesn't mean it's all in vain. All it means is that you're going through a bad patch. You have to expect bad patches. You loved your dog, and he's dead. There are going to be bad patches.

Meditation helps. It helped me, and it might help you. Even if you've tried meditation before, it's worth trying again.

You don't need anything special. You don't even have to sit cross-legged on the floor. You can meditate just as well sitting on a chair. (Apparently it is not a good idea to meditate lying down, because you might fall asleep) All you have to do is find a quiet place, make yourself comfortable, close your eyes and concentrate on your breath. Truly, that's all there is to it.

Okay, so maybe it's not that easy. Concentrating on your breath for fifteen minutes or half an hour takes a degree of one-mindedness that most of us don't possess, at least not in the beginning. Maybe your thoughts wander. Maybe you become uncomfortable, sitting in one position without moving. Maybe you think concentrating on your breath is boring. It is boring, at first. But if you persevere, interesting things will happen. Trust me.

The thing to remember is that meditation is a practice. When people who meditate on a regular basis – once or twice a day – talk about meditating, that's what they call it – a meditation practice. (It is also sometimes called the sitting practice) You aren't expected or supposed to do it perfectly the first time – or even the ten thousandth time. You're more like the itsy, bitsy spider going up the water spout. You try. You fail. You try again. That's why it's called a practice.

Where meditation is concerned, it isn't so much a question of doing it correctly as a question of doing it at all. The biggest challenge is finding the time and making the effort to sit down and meditate for a certain amount of time each day. It doesn't have to be for hours and hours. In fact, it shouldn't be. Some people meditate for 30 minutes, twice a day. Other people meditate for 15 minutes, once a day. Even five or ten minutes is beneficial, and better than nothing. The trick is to do it.

And the best way to get started is to start. How about now? Put down this book, and sit comfortably. If you've got a timer on your cell phone (most do) set it for 10 minutes. Set the timer, close your eyes, and start breathing. There you go. You're doing it. You're meditating.

For me, guided meditations – with music and someone gently talking me through the process – were very helpful, especially in the beginning. You can buy these, or you can download them from YouTube. There are books, as well. Thousands of books. But don't fall into the trap of watching videos about meditation and reading books and articles about meditation, rather than actually meditating. And don't be afraid of experimenting with different techniques. Some people find music helpful.

Others like to use mantras. There's no right or wrong way to meditate. You need to find whatever works for you.

Meditating won't bring your dog back to you, but it will help you learn how to pay attention. Meditation takes you inwards, and that's where you need to be. The future holds endless possibilities and infinite potentialities, one of which is that you and your will be reunited in this life. You need to pay attention to this potentiality just as you need to use intention to will it into existence. Meditation can help. At the very least, meditation is good for you. Within three weeks of starting a regular meditation practice, you'll notice subtle changes. Perhaps your blood pressure will be lower. Or you'll be sleeping better.

But what if nothing is happening? What if none of this stuff seems to be working?

The vibrations are definitely out there. However, the frequencies may be jammed. Human beings seem to have an unfortunate knack for interfering with their own powers of perception. Did you know that only one out of three Americans can look up at night and see the Milky Way? Light pollution has turned our night skies into a yellowish haze. The Milky Way is still there, of course. But most of us can no longer see it.

Consider the countless electromagnetic impulses constantly emanating from your gadgets. Your cell phone vibrates. Your microwave oven vibrates. Your security system vibrates. Nobody has any idea of how this invisible, electronic bath affects the human brain, perhaps because we really don't want to know. (We didn't want to know that smoking cigarettes caused cancer, either)

I suspect that if nothing is "getting through" you may live in a home with smoke detectors, wi-fi, cable television, cell phones, electric toothbrushes, coffee-makers, digital clocks and many other things with little lights that glow all night. Depending upon how old you are, you might take all this stuff for granted, and consider it an essential part of life. You might not realize how new and alien such devices are, in the human scheme of things.

Try to minimize your exposure to electronic gadgets, and see what happens. Instead of carrying your cell phone with you everywhere you go, try leaving it at home or (if you like to have it handy in case of an emergency) in the glove box of your car. Turn off the TV when you're not watching it. Turn off as many of your machines as possible when you're not using them, especially in your bedroom. This will save money, and it will also reduce some of the electromagnetic "noise" that may be clogging the channels.

Continue to pay attention and focus your intention. Keep trying. All you need to do is connect and one day – probably when you least expect it – you will.

CHAPTER 7

Jeannie still thinks I need to get away. "Rocky Point doesn't count. You need to go somewhere new, someplace where there are no memories. Do you know how long it's been since I heard you laugh?"

An hour later I receive an email from Enchantment Resort in Sedona. I have no idea how this got through my spam filters but here it is. Four nights for the price of three. I like Sedona, but I've never heard of the Enchantment Resort, which is apparently famous for its "destination" spa, Mii Amo. I'm not really into the spa thing, because I don't enjoy massages. So maybe that's why I never heard of Mii Amo. But Enchantment Resort's setting is breathtakingly beautiful, and there's a lengthy list of complimentary activities including yoga, tai chi, red rock hikes, wine tastings, cooking classes and cultural evenings. Sedona is only a two hour drive from Scottsdale. Bao and I visited Sedona several times. But we were never at Enchantment Resort so there won't be any memories. Okay, it's not India. But it somehow feels right.

As always, I take Bao's leash and harness along, and the framed photograph. The drive is easy, and the grounds are even more magnificent than in the photographs. The resort consists of a series of low clustered buildings nestled at the bottom of Boynton Canyon and surrounded by four-hundred-foot red rock canyon walls. The canyon is considered a sacred space by the Yavapai-Apache, whose ancestors lived here 8,000 years ago. A rock formation known as Kachina Woman watches over the valley, where the First Woman is said to have sought refuge from a mighty flood and eventually gave birth to the first human beings.

Accommodation for hotel guests is in individual casitas, each with its own private little terrace overlooking jutting cliffs and wooded hills. I explore, wandering down a curved path that leads to a clump of ancient cottonwood trees along the sides of the creek that runs through the valley. Crossing the creek you find yourself at the breathtaking entry of Mii Amo. The spa buildings were designed by Gluckman Maynor, a New York firm that specializes in museums and gallery spaces. It is an amazingly organic structure. The interconnected adobe brick buildings seem to have grown out of the earth. Inside, windows frame stunning canyon vistas as if they are paintings.

Many of Mii Amo's offerings are based upon theoretic diagrams of channels and chakras and acupuncture points that cannot be found in any Western anatomical dissection. Allopathic medicine mostly ignores them, but entire schools of traditional Asian medicine are based upon these metaphysical constructs of the human body because – as anyone who has seen a surgical procedure conducted under acupuncture will assure you – they work.

I discover that Mii Amo is more than just massage. The menu includes Watsu, Reflexology, Bio Aquatic Cranial, Psychic Massage, Past Life Regression and Intentional Aromatherapy, among other things. I sign up for a Signature Facial and a Reiki Healing Attunement. I haven't had a facial in years. And although I don't know anything about Reiki, a treatment that will start "a cleansing process of blockages that can influence the physical body, as well as the mind and emotions" sounds like just what I need.

The perfect dome of blue sky over the soaring red rocks of the canyon evokes pure serenity. This isn't surprising. Sedona is a center for cosmic vortexes, places where the earth's unseen lines of power intersect and create powerful energy fields. Some of these are said to emit electrical energy, which is emotionally, spiritually and physically invigorating. Others give off magnetic energy, which facilitates relaxation. The Boynton Canyon vortex is electromagnetic, where both kinds of energy combine to create feelings of euphoria. I don't know if it's the vortex, the scenery or just getting away, but suddenly everything seems easier, and simpler. This is the "oceanic" feeling of well-being that I've always associated with the sea, but I've also experienced it gazing up at a sky full of stars in outback Australia, and in the sun-dappled silence of a eucalyptus forest.

I return to my room and even though it is quite warm, I sit outside on the terrace for a while, enjoying the clean, fresh air and the silence. I feel very close to Bao, very aware of his psychic presence. I'm discovering that my newfound psychological openness to the nonmaterial forces of the universe is depending less and less upon a belief in reincarnation, and increasingly upon a simple, almost childlike spirituality that seems to draw strength from the sea and the sky and – right now – from the splendid vistas of red rock and vastnesses of blue sky.

Here in the midst of all this natural beauty and stillness, I am close to what Buddhists call a state of mindfulness, the ability to be totally in the present moment. This is what you try to achieve with meditation. Yet without making any effort at all, here I am. I see the clouds. I hear the birds. But I am not thinking about anything. I am simply here. All the channels are open. Bao can feel my energy, and I can feel his. By acknowledging his presence and believing that he will come back to me, I am creating the energy that will draw him back to me. The natural beauty of this place is adding to this energy, reinforcing it. Nature feeds spirituality, if only we'll give it a chance.

It's still early afternoon, and I've put my name down for a complimentary make-up consultation and demonstration. To my surprise, I'm the only one who turns up.

The aesthetician's name is Liz, and she's a dog lover. She shows me photos of her dogs, and I show her my photo of Bao. Although we've just met, I find myself telling her the whole story of his life and death, and my certainty that he will reincarnate. Some people evoke these kinds of confidences, and Liz is one of them.

She brushes her mineral make-up powders on my forehead, cheeks and eyelids as we continue to talk about live and death and reincarnation. Liz doesn't think I'm crazy. She says she has a feeling that Bao will reincarnate, too. And when he does come back, she adds, she hopes I'll bring him to Enchantment for a visit. I don't use much makeup because I don't like the feel of it on my face, but these mineral powders are barely perceptible. I'm delighted to discover that Liz will be giving me my facial tomorrow.

At sunset, I visit the Crystal Grotto, a circular room at the heart of Mi Amo. It has been designed to resemble traditional American Indian kivas, with dirt floors, and a domed ceiling. There is also a central fountain and a spectacular mandala fashioned from petrified wood and crystal. Four large crystals placed at intervals around the room represent the four directions; vanadite, obsidian, selenite and citrine. At the summer solstice the sun shines down through an aperture in the center of the ceiling and strikes the mandala. The Crystal Grotto is used for crystal sound therapy as well as for guided meditations every morning and evening, open to anyone who wants to attend. Group meditations often vibrate with powerful, positive energy. The one I attended certainly did, leaving me feeling calm and confident.

After another meditation the next morning, I go to a yoga class.

I tried a yoga class once, at Jeannie's gym. It took place in a huge, crowded room. An instructor marched onto a stage at the far end the room and began barking out commands like a drill sergeant. "Warrior Two! Down Dog! Pigeon!" Never having done yoga, I hadn't the slightest idea of what was going on. All around me, thirty-somethings twisted, flexed and contorted. The spectacle wasn't remotely spiritual, but it was certainly impressive. I sat on my mat and watched until it was over, but I never went back.

I was assured that yoga classes at Enchantment were nothing like that, and they weren't. That first morning, there are only three of us. Our instructor introduces herself and asks us to sit comfortably on our mats. Have we had any injuries she should know about? "Yoga is about the unity of breath and movement," she says. "Breath is more important than movement. Yoga is not an agility competition. There are many versions of every pose, or asana. The goal is not achieve a particular pose, but to stimulate the invisible, complicated system of chakras and energy channels. The asanas will also to help you look inwards and be totally present. Yoga was meant to provide a pathway to meditation, and mindfulness."

This is different. This is amazing. I love it.

The Cococino red sandstone bluffs possess an intensely spiritual beauty that nourishes the soul. Here, you become aware of the wonder and magnificence of the universe, and of the miracle of life itself. You find yourself moving easily and gracefully, speaking quietly. In this magical place, it does not seem at all impossible that Bao is coming back to me.

Bao is coming back, he is. Our love was so strong. Like Brigadoon. Bao will wake up Buddha. And if he doesn't, I will. I feel better within myself right now than I've felt in weeks.

I meditate in the Crystal Grotto the next morning, and do another yoga class. Then I go for a swim and treat myself to lunch by the pool. I'm more relaxed than I've been in months, and ready for my Reiki Healing Attunement.

My therapist is Mary, an unprepossessing, middle-aged woman with a quiet, vaguely distracted manner. She asks me to tell her a bit about myself. I say that I'm a widow and that I write books and live in Scottsdale. I expect her to ask what kind of books I write, but she doesn't. Instead, she tells me what to expect. "There are three parts to the session – an Aura Clearing, a Reiki Healing Attunement and finally, a hands-on Reiki treatment. You may experience unusual sensations during the treatment, but that is to be expected. If you see visions or images, you must let me know immediately. Do you have any questions?"

I don't.

Mary turns away from me and begins to light the candles scattered about the room. Then she asks me what it was that I hope to take away from our session.

Being unfamiliar with Reiki, I have no expectations and no idea of what – if anything – is supposed to occur. "Look, I'm sorry. But I've never done anything like this. I'm not sure what you mean."

"Well, what do you want to understand about your life?" Mary looks a bit exasperated. "What are you seeking? What do you need to know?"

Okay, then. "I lost my beloved companion a month ago. I think it's one of the worst things that's ever happened to me. I don't want to live without him. But here's the thing. I have this incredibly strong feeling that he's going to reincarnate, that he's already on his way back to me. But then sometimes, I'm not so sure. I just wish I knew." I pause. It was much easier, talking to Liz. "So I guess that's what I need to know. Is he really coming back to me?"

Mary just looks at me, expressionlessly. I have no idea what she's thinking. Maybe she doesn't believe in reincarnation. Maybe she thinks I'm a neurotic nut. There's a silence. Then she tells me to lie down on the table, and close my eyes. As I do so, she dims the lights. There's music. The session begins. I can hear Mary moving around the room. Occasionally she touches my forehead, or my arms. She murmurs incantations in a language I don't know. I lay there quietly, listening to the music.

I don't experience any unusual sensations, and I don't see any visions or images. But suddenly, I feel terribly, terribly sad. My eyes fill with tears, which ooze out and run down my cheeks. Is this what's supposed to happen? Maybe it's part of the healing attunement. But I don't feel healed. I feel apprehensive. I feel a growing sense of unease, like a realization that I've somehow put myself at risk. And this feeling just keeps growing stronger, until it's all I can do not to get up and leave.

Finally, Mary tells me I can sit up. We're done. I sigh with relief. Now, all I want is to be out of here. But Mary is still moving about the room, putting things away. "Did you have any visions or see any bright colors?" she asks.

I shake my head.

"How do you feel?"

"Sad," I tell her. "As if something terrible happened, but I don't know what."

She summoned her spirits, she says. And they came, as they always do. But there was one new spirit she didn't recognize. She describes him as being a man of middle height and medium build, with light colored hair that seemed to be thinning a little bit. And I think he may have been wearing glasses, she adds. "Does this sound like someone you know?"

"It might have been my husband."

Mary seems pleased. "I thought he might have been there for you. But I have to tell you this. When I asked him if he was going to reincarnate, he said he was not. He isn't coming back. Not for the foreseeable future, those were the words he used. I'm sorry, but he was very clear about that."

I'd told her I was a widow, so I guess she thought the beloved companion I'd spoken about was my husband. I could just let it go, but I don't want to do that. I don't know why, but I feel it's important to set her straight.

"It's been 23 years since my husband died. But I wasn't talking about my husband, before. I was talking about my dog. His name was Bao. And I feel so strongly he's coming back to me ..."

Mary's smile vanishes. She looks flustered. "Well," she says, "that's very strange, because I didn't see any animal spirits or pets surrounding you at all. Not a single one."

"No, that can't be right. I've always loved animals, ever since I was a child." Penny would have been there for sure, I'm thinking. And Rosie. And maybe even Valerie and Fudge. And Bao, absolutely. "I can't believe you didn't see any of my wonderful dogs."

Mary is adamant, and she's starting to get cross. "All I can tell you is what I saw. And I definitely didn't see any animal spirits."

I don't want to argue with her. What's the point? I know there hasn't been any kind of positive spiritual connection between us, and I'm wondering if Mary senses this as well. Maybe that's why she's angry. I half expect her to offer me a refund, or at least a second session, but she doesn't. She just wants me to go, every bit as much as I want to leave.

Walking back to my casita through the late afternoon sunshine back to my casita, I feel cheated, and a bit silly. But I don't want to feel like this, especially not here, not in the midst of all this breathtaking, natural beauty. I'm not going to be angry, I decide. Nothing has happened. Nothing has changed.

Spiritual healing isn't like having a tooth filled, and it's unfair of me to dismiss Mary as a fraud. I told her I was a widow, she made certain, quite reasonable assumptions, and she found what she thought I was looking for. She may even been right about Rollyn not reincarnating – "not in the foreseeable future" is actually a phrase he often used. I realize that I should have made it clear to Mary that I was not talking about my husband, but my dog.

I sit on the terrace of my casita, listening to the birds. I'm wondering if Mary really did see Rollyn. That's kind of amazing, when you stop to think about it. But I also wonder why she didn't see any animal spirits. Maybe it didn't occur to her to summon any animal spirits. Or maybe she just doesn't like animals.

I go inside and pour myself a glass of wine. I imagine a bunch of animal spirits hiding behind a bush where Mary can't see them.

You don't have to be a psychic to have spiritual awareness. We are all creatures of light. We all have access to what we need. We've just got to learn how to listen, and how to trust what we hear.

"We are spiritual beings having a human experience," writes Inspirational author Madyson Taylor. "As children, most of us know this, but other human beings who have forgotten what they really are and who cannot help us to know ourselves train us to forget. As a result, we are led to believe that magic is not real, that our invisible play-mates do not really exist, and that we are limited beings with only one earthly life to live. There is enormous pressure to conform to this concept of ourselves and so we lose touch with our full potential, forgetting that we are beings of light ... It is through our connection to this light that we know things beyond what the visible world can tell us, and we see things beyond what the physical world reveals."

That night, Bao comes to me in my dreams. I hug him, and he snuggles close to me and licks my face. *Mary got it wrong. I'm coming back to you. Wait for me. Find me. I'm coming back.*

It's been seven weeks since Bao's death. In the Buddhist tradition, the 49th day following the death of a loved one is particularly significant because at this point, his spiritual essence has most likely connected with his new parents and is finally on the way to rebirth. Special prayers are said on this day, prayers for the blessing of a good rebirth. Today is special. I know this, and have made plans.

After breakfast, I drive to the Amitabha Buddha Stupa, leaving my car in the parking lot and walking the last few hundred yards along a dirt track. There is nobody else here, although other visitors have left offerings of jewelry, coins and water in crystal bowls on the low wall surrounding the stupa. (There's a sign asking visitors not to leave food, because of the wild animals) I walk around the stupa three times, reciting the mantra, Om mani padme hum. I say it 108 times and prostrate in front of the Buddha. Then I write Bao's name in the Prayer Requests Book, and leave an offering. The sheer beauty of the place seems to be a blessing in itself. I feel healed, and at peace.

Whatever you do, Liz told me, don't miss Bob Bear's guided walk to the Indian Ruins. This only happens once a week, on Thursday afternoons. This is my last afternoon in Sedona, and it's a Thursday. Bob Bear is a direct descendant of the Native American tribe that made their home in Boynton Canyon over 20,000 years ago, he tells us, thousands of years before the Ice Age. This raises a few eyebrows. "A hundred years ago, a bunch of archeologists decided that these lands were settled by people who crossed the Bering Sea during the Ice Age. That's not what happened. We were the ones who crossed the Bering sea, going the other way. But they never asked us," Bob says. "So we never told them."

Bob speaks very quietly. You have to strain to hear him.

We follow him through the valley. Set high into the soaring, salmon-colored rock walls of the canyon, we can still make out the shallow caves and eroded remains of the buildings Bob's ancestors once occupied. Probably, the canyon hadn't looked much different to them than it looks to us. I try to imagine what it might have been like living here, thousands of years ago.

It doesn't seem at all unlikely to me that Bob Bear's ancestors crossed the ice bridge into Asia. Prehistoric times hold many mysteries, and when we try to piece together an account based upon what we "know" it is a very slender, incomplete account. A fragment of bone here, a shard of pottery there. We know more about the dinosaurs than we do about ourselves.

At the end of the walk, Bob Bear blesses us all with a special, yellow pollen that won't burn, even if you drop it into fire. Afterwards, I do indeed feel blessed. I think we all do.

As soon as I get back to Scottsdale, I call Jeri. Yes, there's going to be another litter of puppies early in August. Jeri explains that they'd put Sienna with Remington when she came on heat, but when we last talked she hadn't known if the mating had been successful.

"We put them together several times. Sometimes it takes, and sometimes it doesn't. You just never know. And even when we do think it worked, I don't like to tell people we're definitely going to have puppies by such and such a date until I know for sure," Jeri says. "People sometimes plan to give a puppy to someone on their birthday, or on some other special day, and I don't want them to be disappointed. It's not a sure thing. Sometimes you get an ultrasound that shows the dog is pregnant and everything looks fine but then you do another ultrasound and the puppies are gone, because they've been reabsorbed. Nobody knows why. It's just one of those things."

I've never heard of this, but I look it up afterwards. Apparently dogs don't usually miscarry the way humans do, but if something goes wrong (and there are many things that can go wrong) the pregnant bitch literally reabsorbs one or more or even all of the fetuses. One day they're there, the next day they're not. This can happen at any time during the first 45 days of pregnancy, and even later. Right up to the last week, you can't be absolutely certain. Now I understand why Jeri wanted to wait.

Sienna was mated with Remington two days before Bao died, Jeri tells me. However, dog sperm can survive for up to a week in the female's ovarian tubes. I remember being told how hard they tried to bring Bao back after his heart stopped, in vain. Of course they couldn't bring him back, I think now. He wasn't there, anymore. He'd needed to go when he did, to catch his ride.

Jeri is explaining that someone else has put down a deposit on Sienna's litter and that because their check arrived before mine, they have first choice of the females. That's okay, I tell her. Bao is going to be a boy.

"I'm wondering," Jeri says then. "What did your Bao look like?"

"He was blonde, very light. Almost like champagne."

"I don't know if you've seen the picture of Sienna on our website. But she's sort of a reddish color, and Remington is black and white. So there's no saying what color the puppies will be, and of course, Shih Tzu puppies sometimes change as they get older. I guess what I'm saying is that if you want a puppy that's going to look exactly like your Bao ..."

"I don't," I tell her. "I don't have any feeling about what he's going to look like. I have no idea at all. And it doesn't matter. He'll be Bao, and that's the important thing. No matter what he looks like, I'll know it's him."

"There's just one other thing. Our Sienna is a big girl, so her puppies will probably be big, too. So many people these days seem to want a Shih Tzu puppy that will stay tiny. Teacups, they call them. There's no such thing, but that doesn't seem to matter. Personally, I'll never guarantee how big a puppy will grow, because you just never know. But I'm pretty sure Sienna's puppies won't be teacups."

That doesn't matter, either. Bao was big.

Jeri expects the puppies to be born in a few weeks. She promises to let me know, as soon as they arrive.

I'm excited. I call Jeannie and tell her the news. She's just as excited as I am, happy to believe Bao is coming back to me. It doesn't matter that she doesn't believe in reincarnation. Soon I'll have a dog again. A puppy. Jeannie is delighted. "You are just going to love having a puppy," she tells me.

Knowing the puppies are definitely on the way changes things. I am excited and nervous and anxious, in a sort of limbo of expectation. I can't concentrate. I can't settle. I can't even meditate. What I really need, I think, is another one of those yoga classes. Yoga seems to work better for me than meditation. With meditation, you have to make a real effort to concentrate on not concentrating, whereas simply settling my body into the asanas seems to still my thoughts as easily and naturally as water settles in a pond. And afterwards I feel so calm, so centered, so peaceful.

"But it's got to be real yoga," I tell Jeannie. "Not the kind of stuff they do in your gym."

"There must be plenty of yoga studios in Scottsdale. Go and try a few of them. Find one you like."

There are indeed a number of yoga studios around here, but since I don't know very much about yoga, it's hard for me to choose. Finally, I make a list of the five yoga studios closest to where I live. One of them is just down the road, only two blocks from here, part of the LaMar Day Spa. I must have driven past the place a thousand times. I never knew there was a spa there, much less a yoga studio.

It's a warm and welcoming place, from the soothing foyer to the wonderful, tropical indoor swimming pool. I feel instantly at home. At this time of year, there aren't many people around and only two other women have turned up for the Yin class.

Yin yoga is more concerned with relaxing and stretching than with complicated poses. And our instructor – Isabelle – makes it seem so easy, working with each of us, correcting our poses and suggesting alternatives if something is too difficult, or as she puts it, "not accessible". I'd been impressed with the instructors in Sedona, but Isabel is even better. With only two of us in the class, it's almost like having a private lesson.

Isabelle warns us not to push ourselves to our edge. Yoga isn't competitive. It isn't supposed to hurt. "It's okay to feel a stretch. It's okay to feel restless, or even a little anxious. But if you feel sharp pain, tingling or numbness, tell me, and we'll find a better pose for you." She shows us how to use props, blankets and bolsters and styrofoam blocks. And she's chosen beautiful music, which seems to somehow match the asanas.

In Yin Yoga, you settle into a pose, and then you close your eyes and remain perfectly still for several minutes. When you're practicing Yin, somehow, the stillness of your body translates into a stillness of your mind. You stop thinking. You become aware of your body, and your breathing. Meditation is meant to produce the same result, but meditation takes practice. Yin gets you there in minutes. You feel balanced and refreshed and the feeling lasts for hours after you've finished the session.

Isabelle and I chat afterwards, and I explain that I only just "discovered" yoga after doing classes at Enchantment Resort last week. Isabelle wonders what made me choose Enchantment and I find myself telling her the whole story, about Bao's death and how my friend Jeannie thought I should get away and how certain

I am he's coming back to me. I even tell her about the puppies. Isabelle has two dogs of her own, and knows how it feels. Her dog Henry almost died.

"Our vet thought it was the end. Henry didn't know what was happening to him. He was ready to go into the light. But when he heard my voice, he followed it and found his way back."

What a wonderful story! Bao wants to come back too, just like Henry. But he can't do it alone. Like Henry, he needs help. I'm glad I've kept the psychic connection between us strong. I'm glad I didn't give up.

"I really needed to hear that," I tell Isabelle.

I'm still concerned about being too old to take on the care and training of a puppy, but Isabelle – like Jeannie – pooh-poohs that idea. Aging, she says, has more to do with attitude than years. "In yoga we say, You're only as old as the flexibility of your spine."

Isabelle is only a few years younger than me, but the fluidity and grace of her movements is amazing. Isabelle is purely wonderful. I can't believe my good luck. Buddhists say, When the pupil is ready the teacher will appear. Maybe the same is true of yoga.

You'd think it would be easier, knowing that the puppies are about to be born. But it isn't. Sometimes I experience what I call "left brain days" when reason and rationality take over and I wonder What am I doing? How can I even think of starting all over again with a puppy?

So then I go to yoga, and I feel better. Isabelle and Jeanne (the Manager of LaMar Spa) become my friends.

They don't think reincarnation is impossible, or weird. And – like me – they can hardly wait for the puppies to be born. Like most writers, I spend quite a bit of time alone and other than Jeannie – and Judy in Mexico and Lynn in Florida – I don't have a huge circle of friends. Being among people who are sympathetic and caring and don't think I 'm crazy is really wonderful.

Even so, there are bad days. I find the that best way to deal with these debilitating bouts of doubt is to go online and read about people whose dogs have already reincarnated. There ought to be a chat room or bulletin board for people like us, I think. Maybe there will be, someday.

One afternoon, I come across Brian Weiss. It's the Bridey Murphy story all over again, except – unlike Morey Bernstein – Brian Weiss is not an amateur hypnotist entertaining people at a party. Brian Weiss is an eminent psychiatrist, a graduate of Columbia University and Yale Medical School and Chairman Emeritus of Psychiatry at the Mount Sinai Medical Center in Miami, Florida. He uses hypnotism and past-life regression as a psychotherapeutic technique, as do many other practitioners. It turns out that remembering their past lives frequently helps people cope with problems they're facing in this life. I'm amazed that reincarnation has entered the medical mainstream. But apparently, it has. There is even an International Board for Regression Therapy.

Are all these people who claim to remember past lives legitimate? Or are they just recalling long-buried memories? In the beginning, Weiss thought his patient – a woman named Catherine – was fantasizing. At that

WILL YOUR DOG REINCARNATE?

point, he didn't believe in reincarnation. But as his sessions with Catherine continued, the many things that rang true in her accounts of previous lives nagged at him. Even so, he kept reminding himself that he was a scientist, a professional who dealt in facts. Interesting as all this was, he could not bring himself to fully believe it without some kind of proof.

Then one afternoon, Catherine began to tell him intimate things about his own life – things nobody else knew, things nobody could have possibly known. This was the turning point. He'd wanted proof and here it was. Irrefutable proof. Whatever was going on, Weiss realized, it was real. At that moment, he says, he knew his life would never be the same.

Today, Weiss conducts seminars, experiential workshops and training programs in past-life regression therapy for professionals. I spend quite a bit of time on his website. I've never been particularly curious about who or what I was in my former lives, but when I find that he's presenting a one-day Past Life Regression Seminar here in Phoenix during September, I decide to go. I don't expect much. But I'm definitely curious.

HOW TO HELP YOUR DOG REINCARNATE: WEEK SEVEN

In the months after Bao's death, I discovered powers that I'd never dreamed I possessed. We all possess these powers. They lie dormant, inside every one of us. We can tap into them. And when we do, anything is possible. To go back to the crystal radio analogy, it's just a matter of finding the right frequency and tuning in.

But there are many frequencies, and the strength of each signal can vary. My knowledge that Bao was coming back to me ebbed and flowed. Sometimes, it seemed to vanish. Other times, it was little more than a whisper. But on three occasions it was so strong that it filled my soul with an overwhelming consciousness of the numinous and of the limitless potentiality of the universe. That happened on the high plains of Colorado, at the beach in Mexico, and in Sedona.

There is – believe it or not – a scientific explanation for this.

Mountains, forests (especially pine forests) beaches, rivers and waterfalls all generate negative ions. A century ago, Nobel Prize winning chemist Dr. Savante August Arrhenius discovered that when we breathe negative ions, they are absorbed into our lungs and bloodstream and create biochemical reactions that boost the brain's production of serotonin. This produces feelings of happiness and well-being, even euphoria. In addition to making us feel good, negative ions also promote alpha brain waves and increased brain wave amplitude, which lead to higher levels of awareness. Professor of Physiology Dr. Jacob calls them the "vitamins" of the air.

There are tens of thousands of negative ions in the air at beaches, or at the top of a mountain, but there probably aren't very many in the air that's circulating through your home or place of work. Dust reduces the number of negative ions in the air, as does static electricity. Synthetics (building materials, carpets, furniture and fabrics) plastics and urethane finishes further deplete them. If what you see when you step outside is steel and concrete and glass and asphalt, you may need to go someplace else in order to tune in to the rhythms of the universe. It's only recently (in evolutionary terms) that we removed ourselves from our natural surroundings and lost touch with these rhythms. We all need to find them again. Especially you, because this is how you'll find your dog.

Go to a place that's beautiful, according to your own sense of beauty. Some of us love the sea. Others love the mountains, the forests, or even the awesome severity of the deserts. So long as it's natural and peaceful, it doesn't matter. If you have the time and the money, it could be any place in the world. If you've only got a hundred dollars and a couple of days, you can probably find it within a few hours drive.

If you can't give yourself a few days, give yourself a few hours. Most towns have parks. Most cities have botanical gardens. You can often find beautiful, peaceful gardens adjacent to museums, libraries and even hospitals. Even a nursery will work, especially if it has a greenhouse. Park your car and explore on foot. Slip off your shoes and feel the earth under your feet. Close your eyes and take a deep breath and see if you can smell the grass, and the trees. Look up, and feel the sun on your face. Sit on a bench and watch the ducks on the pond. Touch a flower petal, and be amazed at how soft it is.

Even a single hour can be transformative. Meditate at your window, at dawn. Or meditate outdoors, surrounded by the sound of birdsong, or the babble of a creek. Whether it lasts for a few days or only a few hours, reacquainting yourself with the beauty and vibrancy of nature will help you go deeper into your own being.

You can also try to "fix" your home environment to make it more spiritually positive and nurturing. You've probably heard of Feng Shui, the Chinese prescription for living in harmony with nature. Feng Shui is based upon an understanding of **qi,** which is defined as the active energy that permeates the universe, similar to what we call negative ions. **Qi** flows, like a stream. When we follow the flow we are attuned with nature, and the universe. When we struggle against it, we become unbalanced. But as we've become more civilized, say Feng Shui practitioners, we've lost the ability to know if we're swimming with the stream, or against it.

Many of the **qi** blockages within your home that create bad Feng Shui can be neutralized with things like strategically placed indoor plants and mirrors. Running water helps too – which is why you see aerated aquariums in even the smallest Chinese restaurants. Small changes often yield amazing results. An insomniac acquaintance of mine repositioned his bed so that it faced north rather than southwest, and has been sleeping soundly ever since.

You might even consider purchasing a negative air ionizer.

Do whatever you need to do to create an environment where the signals can come through. Be aware of negative ions, and the flow of **qi.** Give the universe a chance.

CHAPTER 8

On the first day of August I wake up feeling distressed and uneasy. This is different. Something is wrong, but I don't know what. As I walk towards the kitchen to make coffee I realize I can no longer feel Bao's psychic presence. He isn't here with me, anymore. He simply isn't here. I concentrate. I try to evoke his presence. But it's no good. He's gone. I pace, distracted. What happened? Where is he? Has something happened to Sienna?

I wait an hour, then send Jeri an email.

She replies almost immediately. Sienna has just had her puppies. Five beautiful babies, one girl and four boys. Mommy is being protective, Jeri writes, so she hasn't had a chance to get a really good look at them yet. But she'll take some photos as soon as Mommy goes out to potty.

The photos arrive just before noon. The five puppies look like little hamsters, with their perfect tiny ears and their perfect, tiny tails. Two of them are black, and the other three are dark brown. I immediately know which one is Bao. He's the one with the blaze of white on his tiny forehead.

I forward the photo to Jeannie, who immediately telephones. "He's the one with the white on his head," she says.

"How do you know? You don't even believe in reincarnation."

"Gail, I'm telling you. That's the one."

The next day, there are more pictures. Jeri holds each puppy in the palm of her hand, and photographs it. They are so tiny! Their little eyes are tightly closed and their little legs are no thicker than Jeri's finger. She always gives temporary names to her puppies, assigning each litter a different letter of the alphabet. The puppy with the white blaze on his forehead is Logan.

Logan doesn't look anything like a Shih Tzu. The pigment hasn't come in around his nose and mouth, and the big, pink muzzle and high forehead make him look like a little chimpanzee. This, I think, is too bad. Bao was such a beautiful little dog. Right until the day he died, strangers stopped us on the street to exclaim over him. Jeannie is disappointed, too. Why couldn't he be one of the pretty ones? she asks.

"Maybe that's what he's supposed to learn in this life," I say. "Everybody can't be beautiful. Maybe he needs to learn humility."

"I still wish he wasn't so funny-looking."

I don't really care. He's here, and he's healthy. That's all that matters.

I'm able to see the puppies for the first time just after their eyes have opened, on August 13th. Jeri and her husband Jackson live in Surprise, in a house made of bales of straw built halfway up a steep little hill a few miles outside of town. Jackson built the house himself. I drive cautiously up the steep, narrow dirt driveway, which ends at a landing. There's already a car and a van parked here, and I'm worried there won't be room to turn around. When I get out of the car, the heat hits me like the blast from an oven. It's a big house, bigger than it looked from down below. The tall grass on the hill rising behind the house is brown and dry. Slowly, I make my way up the flight of shallow, wooden steps that lead up to the front door. They're easy steps, wide and not too steep. Jackson is a good builder.

My knees are trembling. I can't believe this is really happening. Suppose I'm wrong? What if none of these puppies is Bao?

Jeri has heard me drive up, and welcomes me warmly. I'm ushered into a large room full of interesting, wooden cabinets full of curios and various objets d'art. The puppies are in a puppy run that's been set up in the center of the room. They've just had lunch, Jeri tells me. They're always sleepy, afterwards. Mama Sienna wags her tail. She is a beautiful, russet color. Sienna is the perfect name for her.

There's going to be a sign. I'm certain of that. My puppy will do something – I don't know what – to let me know he's Bao. I gaze down into the puppy run. The puppies sprawl comfortably, their little bellies full. One of them is on his back.

"Would you like to hold a couple of them?"

I sit down on the couch while Jeri scoops up Logan and one of his brothers, Landon. Sienna watches, but doesn't bark or protest. I'm surprised how good Sienna is about all this, considering the puppies are still so young and I'm a total stranger. Gently, Jeri positions the puppies in my arms, one in the crook of each elbow. They stir slightly, partially open their little eyes and then go back to sleep. I sit there, cradling two warm, soft, plump little bodies. I can feel their hearts beating. But there's no sign.

I wait. Something is going to happen. One of these puppies will do something to tell me he's Bao. I don't know what. The puppies sleep. Nothing happens. A minute passes. I look down at the puppies and then up at Jeri. They're beautiful, I murmur. And they are. But there's no sign.

Which one is Bao? If there's no sign, how am I supposed to choose? It could be Logan, but it might be Landon. Or even one of the others. At this point I don't know what to say. I am totally at a loss, and I feel like a fool. Maybe it was a mistake, coming to see the puppies so soon after they were born. Maybe I need to go home and come back in a few weeks, when they're older.

Jeri picks up on my feelings. "You know, they can't really do much when they're this young. They've only just opened their eyes, so it's hard to say how much they can see. And their ears are still closed, so they can't hear. They can't bark, and they can't walk. Mostly, they just eat, sleep and potty."

I'm baffled, and terribly disappointed. I'd been so absolutely sure about this. I'd been so certain there'd be some kind of sign. Perhaps this isn't the right litter, after all. Yet it is. I know it is. Then why isn't there a sign?

"Look at that! One of them is kissing you."

I look down. One of the puppies has somehow managed to creep up the front of my shirt to where it's open at the neck and he's licking me with a tiny, pink tongue no bigger than my little fingernail. Not just once or twice, but again and again. He is kissing me. That's exactly what he is doing. It's Logan, the one with the white blaze on his forehead.

"I've never seen such a young puppy do that," Jeri says.

I want to take him home right now. I want to hold him forever and never let him go. But of course, that's impossible.

"They need their mother's milk. And then they need to be weaned. And then they need to learn how to be puppies. You'll have to wait at least six more weeks. Even if I wanted to give him to you earlier, I couldn't. It's against the law."

"Can I come and visit him?"

"If you want. If it isn't too far for you to drive."

We've already bonded. It sounds crazy, but it's true.

"Have you thought about what you're going to call him?" Jeri asks. 'Do you think you'll name him Bao?"

I shake my head. I've been thinking about this and somehow, naming him Bao just doesn't feel right. Bao was Bao. This puppy is also Bao, but in another body and another life. This life will be different from his last life. Each of our lives is different from the one before. I don't quite know why, but I feel that this puppy needs to have his own name.

Cranberry is a possibility. He looks like one of those plump, dried cranberries you sprinkle on salads, dark brown with just a glimmer of red. And Brigadoon, because against all odds, we've found one another again. I like Brigadoon. They're both good names, but neither of them feels right. It needs to be a Chinese name, I think.

The blaze of white on his tiny head looks like a little star. The Chinese word for star is xing. Xingxing. Little star. It's perfect.

Jeri takes several photographs of us together, me holding Xingxing close to my face. She also takes a picture of him sitting on a blue velvet cushion. We arrange for me to come and visit him again the following weekend. It's all I can do to drag myself away from him.

For the rest of the day, I'm walking on air. But Sunday morning, I'm once again dithering and doubtful. A puppy! How am I going to take care of such a tiny, helpless little creature? What if he gets hold of something poisonous? What if he gets trapped under the couch or falls off the balcony? What if he chews through the TV cable and electrocutes himself?

When I check my email, Jeri's photos are there waiting for me. One look at them and my doubts evaporate. He is so beautiful. He is my baby boy. This is right.

Everything is as it should be. Bao has come back to me, just as I knew he would. It'll be fine, I tell myself.

When I go back to see him the following Saturday, little Xingxing is noticeably sturdier, no longer an infant. Amazingly, he seems to know me. The moment he hears the sound of my voice he detaches himself from the rest of the litter and scrambles to the edge of the puppy run, his little tail wagging. He still can't quite walk, but he's certainly trying. In my arms, he snuggles happily and makes little sounds of contentment. The hour I spend holding him and chatting with Jeri seems to pass like a minute.

He's probably not going to look anything like Bao. This doesn't matter, because I hadn't expected him to look like Bao. Now that the pigmentation has come into his little muzzle, he is absolutely adorable, although the black markings over his eyes and around his mouth make him look more like a Yorkie than a Shih Tzu.

This afternoon, I've signed up for one of Isabelle's Mandala Workshops. The concept of the mandala has intrigued me ever since I watched a group of Tibetan Buddhist monks spend an entire week creating a large, dazzlingly beautiful pattern with grains of colored sand. As soon as it was completed – and to the dismay of many of the spectators – they destroyed it. The spiritual force was not in the object itself, the monks explained, but in its creation.

"I'm not artistic," I warn Isabel. This is true. I can't draw, and my watercolors run. Nor have I any feeling for clay, or the potters wheel. Whatever I may have been in my former lives, it certainly wasn't any kind of artist.

"Anyone can create a mandala," Isabel assures me.

There are a dozen of us, sitting around big wooden tables and sharing colored pencils and triangles and protractors, like kindergarteners. You start with a circle, Isabelle tells us. Then, it's up to you.

I lay triangles on top of circles, and place obliques within the spaces, going with the subconscious flow and enjoying the dance of color and shape. I use all my favorite colors, vivid blues and greens and buttercup yellow. Isabelle reads to us as we work, and we also take little meditation breaks and listen to music. I've never done anything like this. I'd found it difficult to imagine, spending two hours drawing abstract shapes on a sheet of paper. To my surprise, it turns out to be rather like meditation. It is also fun.

At the end of the session – after we've all been told to put down our colored pencils – I realize there is one more thing I have to add. My mandala won't be complete until I've drawn these last, squiggly lines. Everyone else is showing their work to one another, and I felt as if I'm being rude, not joining in. But I can't help myself. I have to do this. I have to finish it. Finally, I put down the colored pencil and look at what I've done.

I haven't been trying to draw anything concrete. I've simply been working with shapes and colors, randomly. At least, that's what I thought I was doing. Instead, I've drawn a circle of phoenixes. The phoenix symbolizes immortality, rising from the ashes to be born again, and is one of the most important Chinese symbols, second only to the dragon. And I've drawn twelve of them. They're magnificent. Their wings, their beaks, their heads, their tails – they're perfect.

Pretty amazing, I think. Or as the Chinese would say, auspicious. Isabelle thinks it's amazing, too.

Whenever I feel any doubt whatsoever, I think of my twelve, beautiful phoenixes. Yet I'm still worried about being too old to care for a puppy. Jeannie dismisses this with a wave of her magnificently manicured hand. She's more interested in what I'm doing to get ready for him. If he's going to sleep on the bed, how am I going to keep him from falling off? Is there any kind of animal in my garden that might harm him? And what will I do about the balcony railings?

When I next see Xingxing, he is four weeks old and walking. Well, sort of walking. He'll get up all four legs going, and then suddenly collapse. His ears are open, and I bring along one of his favorite squeaky toys. Jeri thinks he may be frightened by it, but he just looks interested and a little bit puzzled – almost as if he's trying to remember, I think. At five weeks Xingxing is all puppy, responding to the sound of my voice as soon as I walk into the room, nibbling at my fingers with his tiny teeth and wagging that dear little tail for all he's worth. I'd love to put him down on the floor and play with him, but Jeri doesn't allow that. "People come through here all the time," she says. "You don't know what might be stuck to the bottom of their shoes. Their mother's milk protects them when they're babies, but once I start weaning them I just don't like to take any chances."

Jeri tells me Xingxing is the most adventuresome of the group. She'd put the puppies in a cardboard box with low sides, just to give Sienna a break from them. Of course, they all tried to escape, and Xingxing was the first to figure it out. Jeri also mentions she's a little worried about Xingxing's hind legs. He's okay on carpet, but tends to skid on hard surfaces. She doesn't think this will be a problem – he's still only a baby. But she wants to tell me. The puppies will have their first veterinary visit next week, and we'll know more then, she says.

If there's something wrong with his legs, I think, we'll fix it. But there's nothing wrong with his legs.

The Sunday before Xingxing comes home I attend Brian Weiss' Past Life Regression Seminar at the Phoenix Convention Center. I don't know what to expect. Maybe a dozen people sitting in a circle, holding hands and chanting. But I've paid my $139 so I think I might as well go. If it turns out to be as awful as I suspect it might be, I can always slip away during one of the breaks.

I find the room, push open the door and just stand there, dumbfounded. There are hundreds and hundreds of people here. It's a pleasant Saturday in September, in Phoenix. There are plenty of other things to do. And it's not as if we're in a huge metropolis like New York or San Francisco, where there are lots of way-out people. This is Phoenix. Can there possibly be this many people in the Phoenix metropolitan area who believe in reincarnation?

Still amazed, I make my way into the crowded room and manage to find a seat somewhere near the front. As I listen to the conversations around me, I realize that people have come from all over the western United States just to attend this seminar. I strike up a conversation with the woman sitting next to me. She's traveled all the way from Vancouver. I tell her about Bao and Xingxing. She's interested, but not surprised. She knows lots of people whose dogs have reincarnated, she tells me. Cats, too. But mostly dogs. She wonders why that is. The room is filling. By the time the seminar begins, there are nearly thousand people assembled.

Brian Weiss welcomes us, and introduces himself. How many of us have attended one of his other seminars? All around me, hands shoot into the air. And how many of us have read one of his books? Just about everybody, it seems, except me.

He talks about Catherine, the patient who launched him on his investigations into reincarnation and past lives. He'd originally been treating her for depression and hypnosis is often helpful with such patients, he says. So there was nothing unusual about the therapy, or the treatment. He'd done this dozens of time. What was unusual was Catherine's response to it, her recollection of former lives. Catherine spoke of places and people of which she knew nothing in her present, conscious life. It was impossible to doubt her. But it was also impossible – at least, at first – for Weiss to believe her. There was too much at stake. What would his colleagues think if he admitted to believing in something like reincarnation? He had a family, a career and a professional reputation to consider. But in the end, the incredible things he'd learned from Catherine could neither be denied, or ignored. Choosing his confidants with care, he began to share his experience with other psychiatrists and psychologists.

To his surprise, he discovered that many of his colleagues who used hypnosis as a therapeutic technique had had similar experiences but – like him – had been reluctant to talk about it because they feared for their careers and reputations. "Clinicians all over the United States were aware of this," Weiss told us. "But up until that point, they'd just kept quiet."

It's been over twenty years since Weiss wrote his best-selling, *Many Lives, Many Masters*. By now, the idea of past life regression is accepted in most psychoanalytic circles. There is even an International Board for Regression Therapy which has set up courses, guidelines and a journal. Brian Weiss calls it a world wide bubbling up of awareness.

Today, Weiss tells us, we will have the opportunity to participate in several group sessions that will perhaps help each of us to remember one or more of our own former lives. Some of us may gain huge insights into ourselves. Others may experience nothing. And others may think they've felt nothing, only to discover memories of a former life tomorrow, or next week, or even next month. The effects of exercises like the ones we will attempt can be subtle, almost imperceptible. But no matter what happens, or doesn't happen, we need to know there is nothing to fear. Hypnosis is not about giving up control, Weiss tells us. Hypnosis is about focus, and concentration.

We began with an exercise in psychometry, or swapping thoughts. We're asked to partner with someone we don't know and exchange small objects of personal significance – a ring, a pen, whatever we happen have in our pocket or purse. We then sit silently for several minutes, concentrating upon the object in our hand and observing whatever thoughts and feelings arise. Finally, we take it in turns to tell our partner what we thought and felt.

Some pairs have quite remarkable results, but most don't. My partner and I certainly don't. I'm not disappointed, or even surprised. Thought is simply energy vibrating at a specific frequency. Some of us can tune into many frequencies, but many of us cannot. I am one of the latter. But I've always known that.

Nonetheless, I believe that there are people who can heal others – and even themselves – through thought. I believe there are people who have extraordinary powers of extrasensory perception. I believe there are people who can dream lucid dreams and go on astral, out-of-body journeys. I'm just not one of them. Someday I may miraculously tap into the parapsychological powers buried deep inside of me, and be able to see auras and take astral journeys. That would be wonderful. But for now, the miracle of Bao's reincarnation is more than enough.

During the break I feel a gentle tap on my shoulder. The woman sitting behind me says she couldn't help overhearing what I'd said about my dog reincarnating. She's a yogini, from Hawaii. "It's a very nice story," she says. "But this time, you should try not to become so attached."

The attachment thing, again. I don't know what to say. Luckily, the break is almost over and the moderator is asking us to take our seats.

After the break, we're ready for our first Mass Regression. Brian tells us to make ourselves completely comfortable, to feel free to leave our chairs and lie on the carpeted floor if we like. Many do this. I stay where I am, and close my eyes. Having never done anything like this before, I have an open mind, but no expectations.

We are told to cast our minds back to something we remember from our childhood. Then, to infancy. (This and other regressions are available on CD) Now, we are asked to remember an even earlier time, perhaps in the womb. And then, earlier still.

I feel as if I am asleep, and dreaming, I am a young child clinging to the back of a man riding a horse. I am wearing some sort of rough, one-piece garment but my feet are bare. There is smoke and fire and shouting, total confusion. I glimpse faces in the firelight, swarthy faces. The man on the horse has straight black hair that hangs to his shoulders, but that is all I can see of him. I don't know who he is. I don't know who I am. I don't even know if I'm a boy or a girl. What I remember is hanging on for dear life as the horse gallops frantically through the chaos. And then I'm inside some sort of cloth structure, something like a tent. There's a lot of smoke. It's hard to breathe, and very dark. The tent is on fire. I'm trying to reach another, younger child, trying to get him out before it's too late.

I open my eyes.

Perhaps I did fall asleep. Or maybe, I think, I imagined it. This is what most people think the first time they recall a past life, Brian tells us. This is how we've been conditioned, how we've been taught to react to such experiences. All our lives, we've learned to dismiss whatever seems empirically impossible as being imagination, dream or delusion. We medicate people to make them stop having these experiences.

I don't think I imagined it. And I know I wasn't dreaming, because I wasn't asleep. It looked like a dream and felt like a dream, but while I was experiencing it I was simultaneously aware of where I was – sitting on a folding chair, in an auditorium, surrounded by hundreds of people.

There had been nothing in Brian's words to conjure up such an odd and violent succession of images. But I'm confused. The problem isn't that I don't believe in reincarnation. I do. But believing is one thing and coming face to face with a possible previous life – as I have just apparently done – is something else. I need to think about it, so I go off by myself during the lunch break. It comes to me that the younger child is my brother, not the brother I have now but my brother in a different life.

And I also am aware of a subliminal impression of a wild, undulating landscape, open country with no trees.

We do another group regression in the afternoon session, but this one doesn't work for me. Brian tells us to envision seven doors, each of which opens onto a different historical era. Now, he says, choose one of the doors, open it and walk through. But I'm a history buff and when I think of an era, my left brain immediately takes over as I automatically marshall the relevant events, dates, and personalities. I end up with facts and figures, rather than feelings.

It's less than a week until I bring Xingxing home. I lie down on the floor of each room in my condo to get a puppy's-eye view of possible hazards. I hire cleaners. I transform my four-poster bed into a giant crib by taping strips cut from cardboard boxes around three sides. Xingxing will sleep in bed with me, just as he did when he was Bao. I haven't washed the comforter since Bao died, because I want him to be able to recognize the smell and know he's back at home, in his own bed. I've also blockaded my balcony railings with styrofoam blocks fit between the spaces in the railings. Xingxing is still small enough to walk between the railings without even touching them.

Finally, the day arrives. I'm awake before dawn. Everything is ready.

He'll ride home with me in a little basket I bought specially, and lined with a fleecy, flannel blanket.

Jeri is waiting for me. Xingxing has had his breakfast and a bath. He's soft and clean, and smells like puppy. Jeri has put together a little package that includes a supply of the kibbled food he's been eating, a little puppy collar, a food bowl and one of the blankets that's been in the puppy run (so he'll have something familiar to smell) as well as a cute little khaki slouch hat, just for fun. She also gives me Xingxing's AKC papers, and shows me how to complete his registration. Suddenly, it's happening. I'm bringing him home.

Xingxing settles down happily in the basket. He doesn't get carsick, and after a five minutes or so he curls up and goes off to sleep. He wakes up as soon as I park the car and puts his little paws up on the edge of the basket, wagging furiously. Truly, it's as if he knows where he is. I pick him and carry him into the lobby, into the elevator and then down the hall to my condo. Opening the door, I set him down on his sturdy little legs.

We did it, I tell him. You're home.

Xingxing goes straight to his water dish, looks at it, and looks back at me. He's never seen a water dish. Jeri used a water bottle, attached to the mesh of the puppy run. Xingxing dips his little nose into the water, and looks at me again. Good boy, I tell him. He licks the water off his nose with his tiny pink tongue and wags his tail, pleased with himself.

Now he proceeds to the bedroom. He seems to know exactly where he's going. Does he somehow remember? Children remember their former lives, and perhaps puppies do, too. He stops at the foot of the bed and looks up at it, baffled. It's as if he's wondering, What happened? How did it get so high?

He turns and trots back towards me. Then he suddenly turns and heads for the sliding glass doors that open onto the patio. He takes a couple of steps, but it's too late. A tiny puddle forms beneath him. He looks down at the puddle and then up at me, appalled. His little tail droops.

It's okay, I say. You're a puppy. Accidents happen.

We go outside together. Xingxing trots to Bao's favorite spot, and sniffs. He squats again and poops, and I praise him lavishly.

There is no settling in. There is no period of adjustment. Xingxing simply walks back into his life as if he's never left it.

As he grows older, his puppy coat becomes lighter and lighter. By the time he's six months old, he looks exactly like Bao, except for the Fu Manchu mustache.

Nothing remotely like this ever happened to me. Never, in my entire life. I continue to be amazed. Sometimes I ask myself, Did it really happen? Or have I been telling myself this incredible story for so long that I've finally talked myself into believing it?

A passage in Michael Roads' book reads: "If this is an illusion I am experiencing with Nature, if it is all imagination — then it's okay. I like it. Who can make me a better offer? Polluted food and air? Is that better? To maintain a belief in death, fear, greed? Are they better? A dogmatic religion with a judgmental God? Is that better? My experience is uplifting, expanding, loving, creative, intelligent. Who can offer me a better reality or illusion? ... I am not denying the pain, fear, doubt, sorrow of everyday reality, but neither need I cling to such a powerful belief while denying the creative, intelligent love of Nature ... I accept my experience. I believe my experience. I know what I know."

My experience has also been uplifting, expanding, loving, creative and intelligent. I accept it, and I'm grateful for it. Like Michael Roads, I know what I know.

Jeannie insists she still doesn't believe in reincarnation. "But I have to make an exception in this case," she'll tell you. "If a dog ever did reincarnate, it's Xingxing."

HOW TO HELP YOUR DOG
REINCARNATE: WEEK EIGHT

That's my story. That's how it happened to me.
Your story will be different.

The energy and the vibrations exist. It is just a question of tapping into them, and believing what they tell you. Believing isn't always easy, but belief is the catalyst. It's belief that makes things happen.

So keep believing, no matter how difficult it sometimes seems, no matter how long it takes. If you suddenly decided that you wanted to be a concert violinist, you wouldn't expect to pick up a violin and play Mozart. You'd have to start at the beginning. You'd have to practice. But eventually, you'd be able to play the violin.

The analogy isn't perfect, because not everyone can play a musical instrument. However, every one of us does possess parapsychological capacities and capabilities. Some of us are "naturals" but most of us have to learn how to develop our parapsychological powers, just as we have to learn how to walk and talk.

Intuition isn't an effortful thing. If anything, it's the opposite. Intuition is what happens when you let go. We're used to thinking of ourselves as being mind and body. In fact, we are mind, body and spirit.

You've already come a long way. You're consciously thinking about your dog, sending positive energy into the universe. You're keeping a journal. You're meditating. You're becoming aware of your physical surroundings, and of how they impact your perception. You're learning how to be still, how to go inwards, and how to listen to your own, inner voice. You're cultivating mindfulness.

When your dog comes back to you, it will be because your relationship is deep, enduring and karmic. When your dog comes back to you, it will be because you have helped him find his way. Perhaps he'll be reborn. Perhaps he'll swap souls with another dog. Perhaps you'll find him in a shelter or even on your doorstep.

So continue to pay attention. Continue to keep your mind and heart open. Continue to follow your instincts.

If you truly want your dog to come back to you, he will. All sentient beings reincarnate. Every positive thought you think brings him closer. Believing he will come back to you creates the positive energy that will eventually make it happen. The future is a dimension of unlimited potentiality where anything is possible.

It will happen. If not today, then tomorrow. Or next week, or next year. But it will happen.

Your dog will come back to you.

I promise.

Further Reading

Dalai Lama, *The Universe in a Single Atom* Broadway Books, 2005

Cameron, W. Bruce *A Dog's Purpose* Forge Books, 2010

Chopra, Deepak *Life After Death: The Burden of Proof* Harmony Books, 2006

Chopra, Deepak and Simon, David *The Seven Spiritual Laws of Yoga* John Wiley & Sons, Inc. 2004

Myers, Arthur *Communicating with Animals: The Spiritual Connection Between People and Animals* Contemporary Books, 1997

Salzberg, Sharon and Goldstein, Joseph *Insight Meditation Workbook* Sounds True, 2001

Sogyal Rinpoche *The Tibetan Book of Living and Dying* Harper San Francisco, 1992

Roads, Michael *Talking to Nature*

Weiss, Brian L. M.D. *Many Lives, Many Masters* Fireside, 1988

Made in the USA
Las Vegas, NV
13 February 2022

43850699R00111